50 rules
kids won't
learn in school

Also by Charles J. Sykes

Profscam

The Hollow Man

A Nation of Victims

Dumbing Down Our Kids

The End of Privacy

50 rules kids won't learn in school

Real-World Antidotes to Feel-Good Education

• •

CHARLES J. SYKES

ST. MARTIN'S PRESS 🐾 NEW YORK

www.stmartins.com

Design by Sarah Maya Gubkin

Library of Congress Cataloging-in-Publication Data

Sykes, Charles J., 1954–
    50 rules kids won't learn in school : real-world antidotes to feel-good education / Charles J. Sykes.—1st ed.
        p. cm.
    ISBN-13: 978-0-312-36038-2
    ISBN-10: 0-312-36038-X
    1. Child rearing. 2. Children—Conduct of life. 3. Parenting. I. Title. II. Title: Fifty rules kids won't learn in school.

HQ769.S95 2007
649'.1—dc22

                                                                                2007019317

First Edition: August 2007

10 9 8 7 6 5 4 3 2 1

For Janet

contents

● ● ● ● ● ● ● ● ● ● ● ●

Contents

preface
• • • • • • • • • •

There are two things you need to know about this book:

First, the world is full of touchy-feely books of affirmation. This is not one of them.

Second, these rules were not written by Microsoft founder Bill Gates.

I mention this because these fifty rules began as a mere ten rules that I used in a television commentary back in the mid-1990s; they grew to twelve, and then to fourteen*. Along the way, they took on a life of their own, especially after they were somehow attributed to Gates. With that attribution, the original rules raced across cyberspace, showed up in thousands of e-mails and Web sites, and were picked up by newspapers and an assorted collection of politicians and motivational speakers and commentators, including radio's Paul Harvey and advice columnist Ann Landers—all crediting the rules to the Master of Software. This was flattering and a bit exasperating. I enjoyed the fact that so many found the rules valuable, but it was a mixed blessing when my own e-mail box began to fill with the brilliant insights of Bill Gates.

Eventually, the word got out that Gates was innocent of the deed and that the blame rested solely with a guy named Sykes. Web sites devoted to tracking down urban legends actually

---

* See Appendix I for the original "Fourteen Rules Kids Won't Learn in School."

devoted pages to debunking the Gates link. One debunker, www.snopes.com, commented: "Why it's attributed to Gates is a mystery to us; it doesn't really sound the least bit like something he would write. Possibly, the item the Internet-circulated version of the list generally ends with ('Be nice to nerds') struck a chord with someone who views Gates as the ultimate successful nerd of all time." That's as good a theory as I've heard.

But how to account for the enduring appeal of the original rules, which survived being delinked from Gates? I think the explanation is that they were such a blunt contrast to the thumb-sucking, feel-good infantilism that has become so common in American education and culture.

Previous generations thought it was their duty to prepare young people for the ups and downs of life as a matter of course and as an obligation. There is a long and rich literary tradition of books giving sound, realistic advice to young people, written by people who thought it was their job to provide children with a guide to growing up, rather than to amuse and entertain them or to be their buddies. Today, however, children can spend years in the company of credentialed goo-goos who not only miseducate them about the real world but also fail to give them the tools to make their way in it. This book is intended to counter their influence: think of it as a user's manual for the real world.

The themes in this book have been ably addressed by Christina Hoff Sommers and Sally Satel in *One Nation Under Therapy*;[1] Jean Twenge in *Generation Me*;[2] and Michael Barone in *Hard America, Soft America*.[3] I have also drawn on the work of author James Stenson (whose writings, including *Upbringing*,[4] deserve a much larger audience). The rules also draw inspiration from Lord Chesterfield, Anatole France, Teddy Roosevelt, La Rochefoucauld, P. J. O'Rourke, H. L. Mencken, and Viktor Frankl, as well as from a talented group of writers including Lance Burri, Paul Graham, Rick Esenberg, Tom McMahon, and John Hughes. But the primary source has been the ongoing march of folly, inanity, and pabulum in both popular culture and public education; for the constant inspiration, I'm eternally grateful.

I am also grateful for the ongoing support of my colleagues at Journal Broadcast for providing me with an outlet for the early version of these rules and helping me develop some of the issues on my radio show and in my columns. Special thanks to my agent, Glen Hartley, who believed in this book, and to my editor at St. Martin's Press, George Witte, who saw the possibilities of the full fifty rules.

And, as always, thanks to my wife, Janet, who has been my constant counselor and inspiration. For years she has been encouraging me to expand the original fourteen rules and to write this book. Without her it would not exist. I would say that I don't know how to repay her, but I know that she has a lengthy list of ideas and suggestions, many of them having to do with remodeling. I love you always.

introduction
● ● ● ● ● ● ● ● ● ● ● ● ● ● ● ●

Speaking to the nation on the occasion of the space shuttle *Challenger* disaster,* President Ronald Reagan said that the tragedy reminded us that:

> *All human progress is a struggle against the odds. We learned again that this America, which Abraham Lincoln called the last best hope of man on Earth, was built on heroism and noble sacrifice. . . . We think back to the pioneers of an earlier century, and the sturdy souls who took their families and their belongings and set out into the frontier of the American West. Often, they met with terrible hardship. Along the Oregon Trail you can still see the grave markers of those who fell on the way. But grief only steeled them to the journey ahead.*

Heroism? Sacrifice? Struggle? Hardship? Grief? What could Reagan have been thinking?

What about self-esteem? Self-actualization? The power of a group hug?

Somebody call child-protection services. Bring in the grief counselors, because obviously we have to protect the kids from this sort of thing.

---

* At the memorial service on January 31, 1986.

Things have changed in America.

Somehow a nation of confident, self-reliant adults has been replaced by one run by people who think we need to shield children from such evils as dodgeball and tag.

"A child with a rare disease may have to be put in a bubble," Jonathan Yardley once wrote, "but putting the entire American system of elementary and secondary education into one borders on insanity. Yet that is precisely what has happened."[5]

The symbol of our time, however, is not so much a bubble (which has a certain romantic science-fiction appeal) but the more mundane bubble wrap. Instead of preparing children to deal with the inevitable scratches, bumps, and bruises of growing up, our modern-day nannies insist that we should swaddle them in bubble wrap—and not even the kind that you can have fun with by popping.

The modern bubble-wrap mentality assumes that children are so frail and easily bruised that they have to be insulated from . . . life. No losing, no disappointments, no harsh reality checks. But like a child who grows up in a bubble without developing any immunities to the outside world, a child raised in bubble wrap is not prepared for the symptoms of life: failure, frustration, and having to make choices tougher than the color of their new iPod sleeve.

In many ways these are the best of times to be an American child: an age of prosperity, choice, technological plenty, and parental indulgence. When have young people ever been more cared for, deferred to, or pampered? But these also are one of the worst of times, because seldom if ever has a generation been less well prepared to cope with the world they will face. We aren't just failing to make "rugged individuals." We aren't even making competent adults.

In a 2004 *Psychology Today* article, Hara Estroff Marano noted that these frantic efforts to cushion children from bumps may explain the rise of depression and other psychological disorders in what Jean Twenge calls "Generation Me." Marano wrote:

> *With few challenges all their own, kids are unable to forge their creative adaptations to the normal vicissitudes of life. That not only makes them risk-averse, it makes them psychologically fragile, riddled with anxiety. In the process they're robbed of identity, meaning and a sense of accomplishment, to say nothing of a shot at real happiness. Forget, too, about perseverance, not simply a moral virtue but a necessary life skill. These turn out to be the spreading psychic fault lines of 21st-century youth. Whether we want to or not, we're on our way to creating a nation of wimps.*[6]

Author-commentator Michael Barone suggests that the country today is divided between what he calls "Hard America," which stresses competition and results, and "Soft America," which coddles and protects its children.[7] And indeed, there seems to be an ever-widening gap between those two Americas.

One America teaches their kids responsibility, self-control, and accountability. The other America files lawsuits claiming their children suffer from "emotional distress" if they get kicked off the basketball team.

One America overcomes adversity and recognizes that we are all tested by bad times. The other America thinks kids could be traumatized by having their papers marked with red pens.

Where the earliest settlers saw America as a shining city on the hill, the other America sees the potential for a lot of slip-and-fall cases.

In his classic *The Screwtape Letters,* C. S. Lewis wrote:

> *We direct the fashionable outcry of each generation against those vices of which it is least in danger and fix its approval on the*

*virtue nearest to that vice which we are trying to make endemic.
The game is to have them all running about with fire extinguish-
ers whenever there is a flood. . . . Cruel ages are put on their
guard against Sentimentality, feckless and idle ones against Re-
spectability, lecherous ones against Puritanism. . . .*[8]

I suspect that Lewis would easily recognize public education
today. Even as evidence mounts that we have created a generation of smug, self-satisfied, entitled wimps, disconnected from
reality and unprepared for the tests that the world has in store
for them, legions of educationists, therapists, counselors, victi-
mologists, bureaucrats, and parents continue to obsess about
how to pump up the self-esteem and bubble-wrap the feelings
of the younger generation.

This book is dedicated to the proposition that precisely the
opposite is needed: that what young people need today is not
more vague, sappy nostrums about "being yourself" or "following your bliss," but a reality check that tells them that life isn't
fair, they aren't entitled, and the world won't be caring about
their feelings quite as much as Mommy and Daddy do. In other
words, it is intended as an antidote to our culture of compla-
cency and indulgence.

Given all of our anxieties and assorted panics involving
child rearing, it may seem contradictory, even perverse, to suggest that we have become complacent about raising our children. But a culture has to be awfully smug about the big things
to devote as much time as we do to issues like the weight of
backpacks, the onerous burden of homework, and self-esteem-
destroying class rankings. The very triviality of our concerns is
evidence that we think we have the big stuff pretty much in
hand.

Despite the gold stars and happy faces, there is growing evidence that we are falling further behind in preparing young
people for the challenges of the emerging world. American
children continue to lag much of the industrialized world in
both math and science, while the results of recent surveys of

their literacy and knowledge of history, civics, and geography hover between embarrassing and "Oh, my God!"

In December 2005, the National Assessment of Adult Literacy concluded that the average college graduate's reading ability had declined significantly in the previous decade. Fewer than a third of college graduates scored at the "proficient" level in the most recent test.[9] The next month, January 2006, saw more bad news: a survey by the American Institutes for Research found that a majority of the students at four-year colleges couldn't do things like understand the arguments of a newspaper editorial or interpret a table about blood pressure and exercise.[10] The same study found that only 20 percent of college students completing a four-year degree had "basic quantitative literacy skills," which meant they were "unable to estimate if their car had enough gasoline to get to the next gas station or calculate the total cost of ordering office supplies."

Despite warnings from business, educational, and political leaders about lagging math and science skills, both parents and students seem to be snoozing through the alarms. A 2006 poll found that most parents thought that there was nothing wrong with the amount of science and math their children were being taught. Only half of the students in middle and high school thought that understanding science or knowing math was "essential" if they were to succeed in the real world after high school.[11]

Precisely which world do they think that is? The one where technological innovation won't matter? Where they won't need science or math to get good-paying professional jobs? Where they won't need to worry about competition from countries that emphasize higher math skills? Where they won't have to understand complex scientific arguments about things like global warming?

There are obvious practical consequences to this tsunami of ignorance: The 2005 "Skills Gap Report" commissioned by the National Association of Manufacturers found that the vast majority of American manufacturers—90 percent—are experiencing a shortage of qualified, high-skilled employees, including scientists and engineers. The lack of skills, the report warned, is endangering the "ability of the country as a whole to compete in the global economy."[12]

When businesses were asked whether the nation's K-12 schools were doing a good job preparing students for the workplace, an overwhelming 84 percent said "no." As global pressure intensifies, the need of American businesses for more qualified and skilled employees will also become more urgent.

In other words, life is about to become even more competitive than it is now.

"You don't bring three billion people into the world economy overnight without huge consequences," observed Craig Barrett, CEO of Intel, "especially from three societies (like India, China, and Russia) with rich educational heritages."[13]

But the problem is not simply that young people lack the academic skills to compete; there is ample evidence that they also lack the necessary attitudes and values. "Even if schools perform well in their traditional role of increasing math, science and reading comprehension skills," the report from the National Association of Manufacturers noted, "this would not address the top, pressing concern of employers—the need for attendance, timeliness, and work ethic."

In other words: *showing up, having the right attitude, and being willing to work hard.* The lack of those basic assets suggests that schools deserve only part of the blame for dumbing down our kids; parents and the culture as a whole have also had a hand in creating a self-absorbed, sulky generation whose expectations and sense of entitlement are so out of whack with the world they are entering.

So it's not enough to merely change the education system: we also have to change the culture that created the dumbed-down schools that are putting so many students behind. And just as the problem extends beyond the schools, the damage is not simply economic. Evidence continues to mount that the bubble-wrapped generation is also finding itself badly handicapped in dealing with the other major challenges of life, from relationships and personal responsibility to distinguishing right from wrong without a reliable moral compass. And despite the efforts of grown-ups to keep them endlessly entertained and insulated, there are signs that many young people are increasingly unhappy and dissatisfied. Colleges report that the severity of student mental problems, including depression, anxiety, and eating disorders, has been rising since the late 1980s.

For many children raised in bubble wrap, life is turning out to be both overwhelming and disappointing. They were sent forth with grossly inflated expectations and with tools that are wholly inadequate to help them cope with life's inevitable switchbacks and speed-bumps. By definition, expectations can be infinite, especially when they aren't tempered by reality; so the letdowns and flameouts are almost inevitable.

In other words, by pumping their heads full of feel-good mush, the nanny class has set them up to fail—educationally, economically, and emotionally. A recent Pew Research Center poll found that most eighteen- to twenty-five-year-olds thought that getting rich and famous was their generation's most important life goal. Reality will bite hard for a generation that has been raised with delusions of specialness and unrealistic expectations

If all of this seems unduly harsh, I apologize. My intention is constructive: I want to help prepare young people to be responsible, competent, confident, self-reliant, independent, realistic individuals who are armed with the inner resources and the habits of mind to resist the blather and blandishments of the world they are about to enter. I've tried to group the rules somewhat thematically, but they do not need to be read in order, and there is some overlap among them. Some will seem more valuable than others, while others will be downright offensive. (See Rule 21: "You're offended? So what? No, really. So what?") Within the rarefied halls of modern educational nannyism, there will undoubtedly be cries of outrage and indignation.

But, as H. L. Mencken once noted, "In all ages there arise

protests from tender men against the bitterness of criticism, especially social criticism. They are the same men who, when they come down with malaria, patronize a doctor who prescribes, not quinine, but marshmallows."[14]

THE RULES

RULE 1

Life is not fair. Get used to it.

The average teenager uses the phrase "It's not fair" 8.6 times a day. The kids got it from their parents, who said it so often they decided they must be the most idealistic generation ever. When those parents started hearing it from their own kids, they understood Rule 1.

Recognizing that life is not fair is a reality check. Hurricanes, tsunamis, plagues, earthquakes, and famines are not fair. Genetics is not fair. The good guys don't always win. It's not fair that some kids are taller, go through puberty early, or can eat gallons of Häagen Dazs without gaining a pound. It's not fair that your average talentless D-list celebrity makes more money than all the math and science teachers in your school combined, and it's not fair when the moronic suck-up gets the good job—but let's not talk about Congress.

"Life is unfair," author Edward Abbey observed. "And it's not fair that life is unfair."

You can't control the unfairness of the world. *What you can control is the way you react.* How you respond will determine what kind of a person you will become. "Everything can be taken from a man," wrote concentration-camp survivor Viktor Frankl, "but . . . the last of the human freedoms—to choose one's attitude in any given set of circumstances, to choose one's own way."[15]

Usually, complaints about unfairness have nothing to do with justice, but are simply a reaction to finding out that you have to take responsibility for your life; that you are accountable for your actions; that your choices have consequences; that you have to work for money; that you have to fix something you broke; that you do not get rewards that others earned while you played video games. None of this is unfair.

Part of the problem is that so many young people know that they are special—they've been told so for years. They think that they deserve and are entitled to all sorts of self-actualization and perks that go with feeling so good about themselves. Some were under the impression that the "pursuit of happiness" meant that they were going to end up dating Jessica Alba, winning *American Idol*, and driving a Porsche. They will have to get used to disappointment.

In the meantime, when they don't get everything they expected, it seems . . . so unfair.

But failing to get what you wanted is not unfair. Disappointment is a symptom of life, not a sign that the world is ripping you off. World hunger is unfair. AIDS is unfair. Not being able to go to the mall in your skanky T-shirt is not. Your share of the federal debt is unfair; having to turn off 50 Cent so other people in your house can sleep is not. So you have a choice: you can either join the chorus of the permanently whining or recognize that you have to take responsibility for your life and learn to deal with it.

Unfortunately, wrapping children in bubble wrap for much of their lives doesn't really prepare them for coping with unfairness. Friends will let you down, good people will get sick, star athletes will blow out their knees, and jerks will win the lottery while a promising physicist at the very beginning of his career comes down with an incurable, crippling disease that destroys his chances for a normal life.

Stephen Hawking was not born in a wheelchair.[16] The famous physicist was an active child, and even though he wasn't good at ball games, he was able to take up rowing when he went to England's Oxford University at the age of seventeen. He was one of the university's most brilliant students—already recognized as a star—but in his third year at Oxford, Hawking began noticing that he was becoming increasingly clumsy, occasionally falling over for no reason.

Shortly after his twenty-first birthday he was referred to a specialist, who began a variety of medical tests to find out what was happening to Hawking. Doctors couldn't tell him what he had, except that it wasn't multiple sclerosis. They told him that he had an unusual disease, that he would get worse, and that they had no treatment.

"The realization that I had an incurable disease, that was likely to kill me in a few years, was a bit of a shock," Hawking later wrote. "How could something like that happen to me? Why should I be cut off like this?"

How could life be so unfair?

But while he was in the hospital, Hawking saw a boy die of leukemia in the bed next to him. "Clearly," he concluded, "there were people who were worse off than me. At least my condition didn't make me feel sick. Whenever I feel inclined to be sorry for myself I remember that boy."

But it got worse. His physical condition deteriorated progressively. He had nightmares about being put to death, and others in which he sacrificed his life to save others.

"But I didn't die" he wrote. "In fact, although there was a cloud hanging over my future, I found, to my surprise, that I was enjoying life in the present more than before." Even as his condition declined, his scientific reputation began to grow and he became engaged to his future wife. "That engagement changed my life," he remembered. "It gave me something to live for."

After 1974, though, Hawking was no longer able to feed himself or get himself in and out of bed. Still, he managed to continue his scientific work.

But in 1985 Hawking suffered another blow. He contracted pneumonia, and in order to save his life, doctors had to perform a tracheotomy, an operation to open a direct airway through the neck, involving an incision in the trachea, or windpipe. Stephen Hawking, who had endured so much, and lost so much, now permanently lost the ability to speak, and required around-the-clock nursing care. He would have to spend the rest of his life in a wheelchair, physically helpless.

For a while, the only way this brilliant scientist could communicate was by spelling out words one letter at a time by raising his eyebrows when someone pointed at a chart of letters. Eventually, he was able to use a small computer and speech synthesizer to communicate. He has used them to write a book, dozens of scientific papers, and even public speeches.

Hawking is now perhaps the world's most famous physicist. He has three children, one grandchild, and twelve honorary degrees; is a fellow of The Royal Society and a member of the U.S. National Academy of Sciences; and has received many awards, medals, and prizes.

Asked what he felt about his disability and the tragic twists of his life, Hawking responded:

> *Not a lot. I try to lead as normal a life as possible, and not think about my condition,* or regret the things it prevents me from doing, which are not that many. *[Emphasis added.]*

Hawking does not complain that life is unfair. How do your problems stack up next to his?

RULE 2

The real world won't care as much as your school does about your self-esteem. It'll expect you to accomplish something before you feel good about yourself.

This may come as a shock. When inflated self-esteem meets reality, most kids complain that it's not fair. (See Rule 1.)

Someday you will have to deliver—not give it your best effort, but deliver. Whether you will succeed depends on your preparation, your skill, and your confidence. Right now you live in a world where failure might be met with a hug and reassurance. You are about to go into a world where failure will be met with "you're fired," "you're cut," or "you're dead." Your mom won't always be there, and you won't be able complain to a very understanding guidance counselor with a master's degree in self-esteem-boosting rationalizations.

To legions of educationists, therapists, counselors, and PTA members who got a C-minus in their introductory psychology course, "self-esteem" has become more than merely a mantra—it has become an organizing principle, an obsessive fixation on making sure that children feel good about themselves no matter what. The result, believes psychology professor Roy F. Baumeister, is that your generation was raised on what he calls "unrealistic hopes, undisciplined self-assertion, and endless, baseless self-congratulation."

So we get a world of meaningless gold stars, "participation" trophies, inflated grades, and happy faces on work that might otherwise be recognized as schlock. But (the philosophy goes) if we don't ask too much, or set expectations too high, no one will feel bad about himself. Instead of preparing children for the challenges, setbacks, defeats, frustrations, and triumphs of life, we bubble-wrap them.

"Behold the wholly sanitized childhood, without skinned knees or the occasional C in history," Hara Estroff Marano wrote in a *Psychology Today* article titled "A Nation of Wimps."[17] This feel-good mania means that "messing up . . . even in the playground, is wildly out of style."

"Although error and experimentation are the true mothers of success," she wrote, "parents are taking pains to remove failure from the equation." That same attitude explains why you can't be expected to handle something as seemingly harmless as red ink.

"Red is the most aggressive of all colors, and it sets off the fight or flight response," one educationist says. "It meant bloodshed or one of the colors in fire, so a clicker goes off in your head that red means danger."[18] Of course, this was the point of the red ink: It was a warning. All that red was supposed to get your attention and tell you that you had done something wrong.

But in schools across the country, efforts are underway to stamp out the use of red pens for marking papers—in favor of friendlier, more affirming, less scary colors.[19]

"Red just has a connotation," one sixth-grade teacher says. "It just doesn't have a good feeling for kids."[20] That's where purple comes in; theoretically it is a way to tell students that they screwed up without making them feel bad about it.

"You want the kid's attention, but you don't want them to feel like a loser at the same time. Purple is attention-getting without being intimidating." Sort of like getting a hug from a big purple dinosaur who wants you to know that you can't spell to save your life, but that's OK.

Of course, the red-pen banners haven't considered that if

purple becomes the color of correction, nothing will prevent it from becoming the new color of crushed self-esteem. As it turns out, that's really not a problem.

"In fact," says an anti-red-ink teacher from Madison, Wisconsin, "there's a move away from marking up papers at all.

"Writing is very personal. You want to not make them feel bad in any way." Apparently this would include the awful trauma of pointing out to students that they had written incomprehensible, ungrammatical drivel.

So getting rid of red pens makes perfect sense to the sort of person who thinks it's worse to mark a child's paper with red than it is for the child to become an adult who loses a job because he can't write a coherent sentence.

If this catches on, companies might decide not to traumatize shareholders by describing losses as "red ink." Maybe they'll move to something more affirming like yellow, or brown. Judges could decide that sentencing criminals to jail while wearing black robes is too negative. "I'm sentencing you to twenty years to life, but hope you'll appreciate the sensitive way I've accessorized myself in purple."

But here's a tip: if you botch your legal brief, business letter, or corporate report, you're not likely to get a drawing of a smiling purple dinosaur holding a friendship flower on your pink slip (or will pink slips become purple too?).

The reality that the self-esteem movement ignores is that children learn to feel good about themselves by actually acquiring skills: this is called self-confidence. Ask yourself if it is better to *feel good* about your swimming abilities, or to actually *know* how to swim.

A Red Cross swim program in Canada gently assured parents that it took a compassionate and expansive view of swimming.

"We acknowledge that children's physical abilities develop at different rates, and the program will *focus on participants' successes rather than areas for improvement*." [Emphasis added]

Alarm bells went off for one parent, who observed:

Excuse me, Red Crossers, but how are my kids supposed to improve their swimming skills if you intend to focus only on their previous successes and not on the areas that need work? [Emphasis added] "Johnny, we're not going to work on teaching you to tread water longer [a skill that would possibly be useful if little Johnny goes on an unsuccessful summer boating trip at the lake]. Instead, I'd like to congratulate you for a fine job of getting your face wet, and beautiful rhythmic breathing, last week."

I thought I was signing them up for swimming lessons, but it sounds as if the Red Cross is more interested in bucking up their self-esteem. No one at the Red Cross . . . seem to have noticed that children derive oodles of self-confidence—which comes from within, rather than self-esteem which is imposed from without— from making marked improvement in any area. On their own! Without gold stars or stickers at every turn! Shocking![21]

A growing body of evidence suggests that this obsession with self-esteem does not derive from an especially profound insight into human behavior. It is in fact a silly notion adopted as a passing fad by the kind of people who used to buy snake oil and fake moon rocks. It is certainly not supported by research or experience. Four scholars debunked the entire notion in a *Scientific American* article entitled "Exploding the Self-esteem Myth," which concluded that despite the national preoccupation with making children feel good about themselves, self-esteem didn't lead to academic success, cure any significant dysfunctions, or prevent bad behavior.[22]

As Christina Hoff Sommers and Sally Satel noted, "High school dropouts, shoplifters, burglars, car thieves, and even murderers are just as likely to have high self-esteem as Rhodes Scholars or winners of the Congressional Medal of Honor."[23] Other studies have shown, for instance, that "bullies showed less anxiety and were more sure of themselves than other children."[24]

The reality is that a movement designed to raise a generation of well-adjusted, introspective individuals has instead helped spawn packs of self-absorbed, navel-gazing narcissists, who often find themselves unable to handle the setbacks of normal daily life. A steady diet of "I love myself because" can create a generation of smug, arrogant, touchy kids who have an inflated sense of their own abilities and worth, but are unprepared to handle adversity. Interestingly, the "experts" never saw it coming. But as one study remarked with notable understatement, "People who have elevated or inflated views of themselves tend to alienate others."[25] Maybe because they are stuck-up jerks.

RULE 3

Sorry, you won't make sixty thousand dollars a year right out of high school. And you won't be a vice president or have a company car. You may even have to wear a uniform that doesn't have a designer label.

You might be under the impression that your new employer is patting himself on the back at his great good fortune in finding such a special employee as you, God's own gift to the workforce.

More likely, he's asking, "What the hell?"

"We're seeing an epidemic of people who are having a hard time making the transition to work, kids who had too much success early in life and who've become accustomed to instant gratification," says Dr. Mel Levine, a pediatrics professor at the University of North Carolina Medical School.[26] The collision of unrealistic expectations with the reality of the workplace, reports *The Christian Science Monitor,* has led to an upsurge in the number of college graduates seeking out "life skills consultants" when they don't "score the good life right away."[27]

One disappointed graduate explained that he had shelled out cash for a "life skills conference" because "things haven't worked how I planned, which has been somewhat eye-opening to me." He had taken a job in radio marketing, but quit because he didn't advance as fast as he had expected. No, they didn't make him vice president of programming after six months, which was both unacceptable and anxiety-provoking. Thus the life-skills consultants.

Of course, teaching "life skills" used to be the role of parents and teachers. . . . That was, after all, pretty much the point of child rearing and sixteen years of schooling. But the growth of the life-skills industry would suggest that something got lost along the way.

"This group isn't about hard knocks," explained Trudy Sopp, the founder of the Centre for Organization Effectiveness. "It doesn't surprise me that they would seek advice, because they don't have a lot of experience." This would include experience making their own decisions, meeting objective goals, dealing with supervisors, getting honest feedback about their performance or lack of it, and encountering and overcoming adversity. "They're told to conquer the world, to shape their dreams," one analyst told *The Monitor*, "but they're not always told to expect these ordinary challenges."[28]

What they do have, however, are expectations. "It seems they want and expect everything that the 20- or 30-year veteran has the first week they're there," says a restaurant consultant.

They don't get it. Instead, employers complain about the lack of "basic employability skills" like having a work ethic and showing up on time, or even showing up at all. This probably shouldn't come as a surprise, since the educationist establishment is often as interested in teaching such skills as it is in having teachers work in July and August or pay for their own health insurance.

The group Public Agenda found that only 37 percent of education professors—the people who are responsible for preparing young teachers—said they thought that maintaining discipline and order in the classroom was "absolutely essential." It gets worse. Only 19 percent thought that stressing grammar, correct spelling, and punctuation was essential, while only 12 percent of the education profs thought that expecting children to be on time and polite was essential for prospective teachers.[29]

And what young teachers aren't taught, they don't learn, or

expect from their own students, so the transition to the world of work is often a painful surprise for everyone involved. "We're surprised we have to work for our money," a twenty-four-year-old writer told *USA Today*.[30]

Welcome to life.

RULE 4

You are not entitled . . .

. . . to a forty-two-inch plasma screen TV with surround sound, a Porsche Boxter, a video iPod, a cell phone with limitless text-messaging and blue tooth, a condo with a pool, a laptop computer, a DVR, the double latte with cream, a Ferrari, or the new Michael Jordan running shoes.

You are also not entitled to everything your parents have, or everything you see on TV or in magazines. You'll have to work for all of it. And then figure out how to pay for it.

This might come as a rude shock to the Generation Me members who get their lifestyle tips from MTV and who have become a modern-day wealth-without-responsibility adolescent aristocracy.

Author Charles Stenson describes a scene at the court of Versailles on the eve of the French Revolution:

> _Young aristocrats stroll idly or lounge about, looking like bored children in search of amusement. They pay no taxes and assume no real social responsibilities; their only usefulness to society is to spend unearned income. They are out of touch with the pressing social, political, and economic problems of the day. They have immediate access to food, drink, musical entertainment, games, and amusements whenever they wish. They also have scarcely impeded access to drugs and promiscuous sex._

Both sexes wear eye-catching hairstyles and colorful clothing bedecked with expensive jewelry. Some, as an ironic lark, sport the clothing of the working classes, also decorated with gold and silver trinkets. Their idle conversation, punctuated by childish laughter, centers around past or upcoming dances, concerts and parties. They also gossip about each other's fashions, antics, and sexual pairings off. From hearing their chatter, one would guess that their only real fears consist of social ostracism, growing old, sexually transmitted diseases and boredom.

Stenson notes that "this picture of life among the tiny elite of the wealthiest classes could also describe the lunch-hour scene at most large, suburban high schools—or Saturday afternoon at most suburban American shopping malls, or a warm spring afternoon at college campuses."[31]

Except that now you have credit cards, and, in case you haven't figured it out, that's going to be a problem. Despite your sophistication about style, technology, and lifestyle, the collision between your generation's entitlement mentality and its tofu-headed ignorance of how money actually works leaves a very nasty mess. By some estimates, teen spending may top $190 billion this year or next[32]—eclipsing the gross domestic products of many countries where people have to go to work to earn money. Most of the money spent by teenagers comes from Mommy and Daddy. Fifty-eight percent of teens (ages twelve to seventeen) say they get money from their parents; only 21 percent report having part-time jobs. (Girls tend to be even more reliant on the bottomless checkbooks of the parental units: 68 percent say they get their money from their parents.)[33]

But Mommy and Daddy won't always be there to pick up the tab.

"This is a generation that has a razor-thin margin of error," says Robert D. Manning, author of *Credit Card Nation*. The problem is that you want all the stuff you want without being able to pay for it. On graduation, they hand you a diploma and a stack of bills. A 2005 *BusinessWeek* report found that the median debt for college graduates in 2004 had gone up more than 66 percent since 1993.[34]

Even so, your peers don't cut back, because that would involve going without, postponing gratification, dropping out of the culture to which they have become accustomed. "My lifestyle was a little out of whack," one debt-riddled graduate told *BusinessWeek,* explaining, "I expected to be able to live the way my parents raised me."[35] Those parents, of course, had worked for years to reach that standard of living. She expected it right out of college, only to find that even a college degree didn't immunize her from an increasingly competitive global economy. Disappointment and debt ensued.

Previous generations understood the "Micawber Principle," named after the character in Charles Dickens's *David Copperfield,* who says, "Annual income twenty pounds, annual expenditure nineteen nineteen six, result happiness. Annual income twenty pounds, annual expenditure twenty pounds ought and six, result misery."

But this appears to come as a surprise to your generation. A 2006 study by the Jump$tart Coalition found that high school seniors would score a solid "F" on a basic test of financial literacy.[36] Even if it's written in a nonthreatening color like purple, the average score of 52.4 suggests an almost militant ignorance about how dollars move around.

One of the questions on the test read:

"Kelly and Pete just had a baby. They received money as baby gifts and want to put it away for the baby's education. Which of the following tends to have the highest growth over periods of time as long as 18 years?"

44.8 percent said a U.S. govt. savings bond
34.8 percent said a savings account
6.3 percent said a checking account

And only 14.2 percent correctly picked stocks, "in spite of the fact that there has never been an eighteen-year period when this was not true."

Less than one in four understood that interest on savings accounts is taxable if income is high enough. Only about 40 percent realized that they could lose their health insurance if their parents lost their jobs. And only 38 percent knew that "retirement income paid by a company" is called a pension.

So you probably also need to be told that FICA is Social Security. You'll want to know that when you find how much it takes out of your paycheck. And no, you probably won't ever get the money back. Here's another reason to learn math: people who don't learn it end up thinking that Social Security will take care of them in their old age. But we baby boomers have other plans for that money. Sorry.

RULE 5

No matter what your daddy says, you are not a princess . . .

. . . even if Daddy throws you a sweet-sixteen party complete with limousines, flights to LA for shopping, caviar, foie gras, shrimp, vases of hydrangeas, chicken wings, beef au poivre, ball gowns, videographers, live bands, and expensive new cars as gifts.

Chronicling the ongoing saga of parental indulgence, *USA Today* recently noted the growing popularity of five- and six-figure teen parties, including a forty-thousand-dollar party in Phoenix that required turning a backyard into a gym—complete with wood floors, bleachers, and basketball hoops.[37] "I feel like a princess," enthused another sixteen-year-old girl, whose party was held at New York's Waldorf-Astoria Hotel. One party organizer told the newspaper that the most lavish parties are usually thrown by parents who weren't rich as children but who now "want to give to their child." And they are giving it to them good and hard.

One pampered high school sophomore who was featured on a popular MTV show devoted to the sweet-sixteen party circuit not only declared, "I'm a princess," but shared these other observations on life:

"I'm such a rock star that I can do this."

"So many people are so jealous of me because my dad owns three car dealerships and we have a lot of money."

And, of course:

"I always get exactly what I want."

The lavish parties have become so popular that in 2006 Hyatt Resorts announced a special program called the "HyaT-Teen Suite 16" to cash in on the pampered princesses and their indulgent parents.[38] Touting "the ultimate Sweet 16 sleepover party" at resorts in the continental United States, Hawaii, and the Caribbean, Hyatt explained that it was recognizing what it called "a trend toward unique 'coming of age' parties that mark celebratory milestones"—like turning sixteen—for children for whom a mere party with cake and ice cream would be unbearably lame. The standard "Suite 16 Package" includes:

- Birthday Concierge consultation
- One night's luxurious accommodations in a two-bedroom suite, for up to 2 adults and 6 guests under the age of 18
- Limo transportation provided, to and from the resort, for up to a 30-mile distance
- One plush Kashmere Spa Robe for the birthday teen
- Use of a digital camera while at the hotel and commemorative picture frame for birthday teen to take home
- Dinner for eight catered by in-room dining
- Special birthday dessert
- Bowls of popcorn and candy
- Movie night in room
- Use of Cranium® games in room
- Continental breakfast for eight served by in-room dining morning of departure

All of this was designed, Hyatt carefully explained, for the discerning, demanding teenagers who "want unique travel experiences that are tailored with their preferences in mind." Carefully avoiding judgmental terms like *spoiled* and *brat,* Hyatt deploys popular cultural buzzwords to dress up all of this wretched excess. "The new package," Hyatt's flacks explained, *"empowers teens*—a new market focus for Hyatt Resorts—*to assert their independence* and celebrate their birthdays by indulging in a range of fun activities—from chocolate manicures to surfing lessons—with their best friends." [Emphasis added.]

This undoubtedly marks the first time that chocolate manicures have been described as *empowering.* But even that stroke of psychobabble pales next to the claim that letting Daddy pay thousands of dollars for a lavish resort party is a way for teenagers to *assert their independence.* Once, teens asserted their independence by listening to unacceptably loud music, by protesting the war, or even by getting a job. Now they do it by getting a facial and charging it to Daddy's gold card. *Viva la Revolución!*

Of course, all of this sets the bar awfully high for the princess wannabes. If this is what she expects from a sweet-sixteen party, what will her high school graduation have to be like? Her college graduation? Her wedding showers? Her wedding itself? Her honeymoon? Baby showers? Anniversary parties?

The princess had better hope that (1) her parents either continue to foot the bill or leave her a boatload of money in their wills; (2) she marries very, very well; (3) she wins the lottery; or (4) she founds a company that comes up with a solution to global warming, a cure for cancer, or an explanation for Britney Spears' marriage to Kevin Federline. Otherwise, life is likely to be a letdown.

Try, for example, to imagine what lies in store for a sixteen-year-old named Marissa who was recently featured on MTV and in a profile in *The Arizona Republic.*[39] Reporter Jaimee Rose notes that, even though Marissa hasn't appeared in anything bigger than the local community theater, her parents have hired a staff of twelve for their little girl: a manager, a publicist, a voice coach, a makeup artist, a hairstylist ("willing to jet off whenev, wherev"), a Web master (what modern princess would be caught dead without her own Web site?), a photographer (who also does Lindsay Lohan), two acting coaches, and a "guy who listens to Marissa humming on a tape recorder, and then puts the music on paper."

"She's spoiled," her mom says, "but hopefully, *it's a grounded spoiled.*" [Emphasis added.] This is perhaps a reference to the grounding influence of the Jacuzzi tub in her princessville bedroom, or the "iridescent-tiled vanity, Chanel bags peppering the careful closet and drapes above the bed, Sleeping Beauty–style."

Marissa describes her work ethic—what it takes to get Daddy to buy her everything she wants—this way: "You know, I just bat my eyes and smile and act really sweet, that's the only way I can get anything."[40]

On the MTV show featuring her party, Marissa gushed: "I know that this party cost over $150,000. My daddy likes to spoil me, so he thinks I'm worth it."

Someday she may find out that not everybody shares his opinion.

RULE 6

No, you cannot be everything you dream . . .

. . . unless you have the talent, education, and commitment to work for it.

Despite the almost-constant mantras of the esteem-builders, you won't necessarily be your own drummer or follow your bliss. Heredity, effort, stamina, intelligence, and education all play a role in defining what is possible for you. I am a klutz, no amount of practice or study would have made me a ballet dancer. Someone who is tone-deaf isn't going to be the next Christina Aguilera or Jewel; someone born with poor eyesight is unlikely to be a fighter pilot. Not everyone who wants to be a Marine will make the cut; not everyone who dreams of being a surgeon will—or can—make it.

This may be self-evident, but the mantras also contribute to false expectations and a sense that life is unfair when reality sets in. Compared with the possibilities you would have had in past ages, your choices are nearly infinite . . . there are no social-class limits, caste systems, or (in general) family obligations dictating your course through life. But students who skip courses in biology and chemistry and fail to turn in their homework still somehow imagine that they can be heart surgeons as long as that is their dream. It's not going to happen.

Students who can't do math won't be engineers, and kids

who don't master science won't be knocking down any doors in
Silicon Valley.

Even so, all the vaporing about "dreams" might explain the
remarkable disconnect between the aspirations of so many
young people and their own abilities, attitudes, and efforts.

Unfortunately, most parents and students seem to be stuck
in denial.

A 2003 survey by Public Agenda found that students, parents,
and teachers were confident that high school graduates were prepared for the workforce. Sixty-seven percent of high school parents were certain their little Ashleys and Kevins would have the
skills to succeed at work; 78 percent of teachers were also confident that graduates were ready for work. If only it were so.

Fewer than half of the actual employers surveyed—41
percent—said that the young people they encountered had such
skills.[41]

The same study also found that 67 percent of parents, 77
percent of teachers, and 73 percent of high school students as-
sumed that a high school diploma meant that graduates had basic skills.

But large majorities both of employers who hired the graduates and professors who taught them scoffed at the notion.
More than two-thirds of college teachers—68 percent—and 58
percent of employers thought that the diploma was no guarantee
that students had mastered even basic academic skills.

So by all means dream big, but realize that your success will
be determined, not by your dreaming, but by your hard work,
study, and perseverance.

RULE 7

If you think your teacher is tough, wait till you get a boss. He won't have tenure, so he'll tend to be a bit edgier. When you screw up, he's not going to ask you how you feel about it.

While we're at it, few jobs foster your self-expression or help you find yourself. Fewer still lead to self-realization.

We've all heard about the sweatshoplike rigors that children endure these days: the stress, the anxieties, the crushing burden of homework, heavy backpacks, the trauma of last year's jeans. Get a grip. Unless you are about to jump out of an airplane over Afghanistan, nobody wants to hear about your backpack; and, come to think of it, the guys who jump out of planes are the last ones to whine.

In 2003, the Brookings Institution examined the notion that U.S. schoolchildren were suffering from a growing homework load that was robbing them of their childhoods. The alleged crisis was plastered across the media; there was even a cover story in *Newsweek* magazine.

But according to data analyzed by the Brown Center on Education Policy at Brookings, almost all of the stories were wrong. In fact, the great majority of students at all grade levels now spend *less than an hour a day studying,*[42] or about a quarter of the time they spend text-messaging things like, "I don't know, what do *you* want to do tonight?" to one another.

A 1997 Public Agenda study also suggested that our schools were something less than sweatshops: Half of the teenagers told researchers that their schools did not challenge them to do their best work. Seventy-nine percent said they would "learn more if schools enforced being on time along with the completion of homework."

Said one teen: "You can just glide through. You can copy somebody's homework at the beginning of the period. I mean you can do whatever you want. . . . They practically hand you a diploma."[43]

Here's a heads-up: this is all about to change, if not at college, then in the workplace, where your new boss is already in a bad mood. Your boss has a boss, who expects results. And the competition is getting tougher all the time. You are not competing with kids from Akron or Rio Linda. You're up against graduates from Singapore, China, Thailand, and Russia, who didn't grow up lying awake at night worrying about the trauma of seeing their papers marked with red ink.

So your boss won't be quite as likely as your teacher may have been to give you as many times as you need to get the job done right; won't let you substitute a diorama or an interpretive dance for writing a brief, making a sale, or getting the job done on time.

One of the differences between the soft world you've spent most of your life in and the Hard America you'll encounter one of these days—is tenure, a rule that basically means that no matter how badly you perform or how shoddy your products, you can't be fired.

Former education secretary Bill Bennett used to observe that there were more consequences for serving bad hamburgers than for miseducating thousands of children. In some urban schools less than 10 percent of the students read at grade level. Odds are that not a single adult will lose his job over this. Over a seven-year period, for example, only 44 of 100,000 tenured Illinois teachers were fired. During a five-year stretch in the 1990s, only 62 of California's 220,000 tenured teachers were dismissed.[44]

If you make a bad hamburger, you will go out of business; if you screw up a classroom, you can become a principal; if you screw up a school, you can become a district superintendent; if you screw up an entire district, you can become an "educational consultant." These are folks who come from a world where having the right letters after your name gives you a lifetime hall pass to avoid actually solving any problem or achieving anything. And just in case anybody notices this, they like to give themselves awards of every imaginable sort, signifying pretty much nothing, except that they know how to pacify school boards and overawe parents, children, and taxpayers.

Former New York City school boss Rudy Crew described the ongoing problem of juggling incompetent tenured principals as "the dance of the lemons."[45] The current chancellor, Joel Klein, notes that in the last two years New York City fired a grand total of two teachers out of eighty thousand for incompetence.[46]

Even in cases of sexual misconduct, it can take years and hundreds of thousands of dollars to get rid of a teacher with tenure. In one famous case, it took six years to get rid of a teacher who had sent sexually oriented e-mails to a teenage girl. While the firing process dragged on, officials had to keep the teacher on the payroll, but out of the classroom. It is so hard to fire a teacher, admits Klein, that the city spends twenty million dollars a year on teachers who spend their days in what is known as "rubber rooms," where they can't do any harm to themselves or others. They sound like good places to put the people who came up with this system in the first place.

But tenure is not the only problem. Says New York's Klein, "We tolerate mediocrity." Because of lockstep union contracts, "people get paid the same, whether they're outstanding, average or way below average."[47] Not only are there few consequences for failure; there are virtually no incentives or rewards for success.

This systemic failure doesn't mean that teachers don't work hard or don't have a lot of pressure: they do. Most teachers want their students to do their work and perform at an adequate level.

But this sort of pressure is very different from knowing that if your employees don't perform, you might have to sell the house and move in with your wife's parents.

The paradox here is that we have entrusted the preparation of young people who will enter an increasingly competitive world to people who have effectively insulated themselves from the consequences of failure.

RULE 8

Your navel is not that interesting. Don't spend your life gazing at it.

The British philosopher John Stuart Mill once observed that the best way to avoid being depressed is to avoid being self-absorbed. The only people who are happy, he wrote, are those "who have their minds fixed on some object other than their own happiness: on the happiness of others, on the improvement of mankind, even on some art or pursuit followed not as a means, but as itself an ideal end. Aiming at something else, they find happiness by the way."

In other words, you won't find happiness curled up with the lint in your navel. As Sommers and Satel have documented in great detail, America is besieged by "a vast array of therapists, self-esteem educators, grief counselors, work-shoppers, healers, and traumatologists" encouraging you to look for it there.[48] But as absorbing as navel picking might be for the practitioners of the various kinds of kumbayaism, it rarely results in courageous or self-reliant adults

At one time such groups as the Girl Scouts prepared young women for the challenges and rigors of life, but even the scouts seem to have succumbed to the cult of self-obsession. Lest young girls be ground under by the anxieties of pushing Caramel deLites and Reduced Fat Lemon Pastry Cremes, the Girl Scouts have unveiled the "Stress Less" badge, which is described as designed "to help girls cope with the pressure-cooker conditions confronting even young children today."[49]

In this case they are talking about the "pressure-cooker conditions" of being eight or nine years old. The program is designed to bring the therapeutic advantages of foot massages, aromatherapy, deep-breathing exercises, worry stones, and stress squeeze balls to preadolescent girls.

All of this is supposedly more stress-relieving for eight-to-ten-year-olds than, say, swimming, hiking, or actually doing anything constructive at all. But that may be beside the point, since the "stress-reduction badge" seems less a counter measure against the wrenching pressure of fourth grade than the projection of the mommys' own very adult, very particular anxieties. The nervous mom of an eleven-year-old confided, "My goal as a mom was to just lift the stress off her."[50] Note: Not to teach her how to cope with the stress, or to deal with it, or to work through it on her own. But to *lift it off her*. And what better way than to go to the spa! According to one newspaper account, one girl named Claire helped "earn" her stress-reduction merit badge by giving her mother a creamy avocado facial and a back rub.

Other merit-badge activities included "smoothing peach-scented lotion on her hands, keeping a journal of her happy and sad moments, meditating in a yoga position, burning an ocean-scented candle, dancing around the room to upbeat music and analyzing her daily schedule."

Sure to come: the Spoiled Suburban Princess Merit Badge.

This obsession with feelings means that even opportunities for children to think about people other than themselves—for example, the victims of the terrorist attacks of September 11 and the aftermath—are turned into more occasions for navel gazing.

Lest children be tempted to focus too heavily on the courage of the heroes of that day—policemen, firefighters, rescue workers, and those inside the World Trade Center towers who tried to help the injured and disabled—one organization named the Families and Work Institute created a program encouraging children to ask, "What's Special About Me?"[51]

Last year, as we watched the events of September 11th, one of the things most people felt very good about were all the people who helped in the rescue and recovery. We saw the police and the firemen, and we liked them because they were so brave. One of the things we don't often pay much attention to, though, is liking ourselves.

And in case children might be tempted to think about what they owe other adults in their lives, the lesson continued:

We know that we like the police and firemen because they are there to help us when we are in trouble. We like our mother because she is so kind, or our big brother because he can fix things, or our grandmother because she is such a good cook and makes us the special things that we like to eat. But I bet most of you haven't thought very much about the things you really like about yourself.

In the days after 9/11, "child-trauma experts" told New York's public school teachers to "avoid clichés such as 'Be strong' and 'You are doing so well. . . . ' "[52]

But, as Sommers and Satel noted, " 'Be strong' is a vital life lesson, not an insensitive cliché."[53]

RULE 9

Your school may have done away with winners and losers. Life hasn't.

In some schools, failing grades have been abolished and class valedictorians scrapped lest anyone's feelings be hurt. Effort is as important as results. This, of course, bears not the slightest resemblance to real life, which still rewards excellence and delivers a sharp poke in the eye to failure.

Despite the wishful thinking of the therapists, counselors, and moon-rock peddlers, life does involves competition, with winners and losers. Some people get hired. Some don't. Some get promoted. Some don't. Some pass the bar exam. Some don't. Some get admitted to the college of their first choice. Some don't.

There's an *Alice in Wonderland* quality to much of public education these days: "Everyone wins, and all must have prizes!" Or at least trophies of participation. In the movie *Meet the Fockers,* the "Wall of Gaylord" celebrates one character's lifetime achievements in mediocrity, prompting the character played by Robert De Niro to muse, "I didn't know they made ninth-place ribbons."

Of course they do. America's closets are stuffed with meaningless trophies, ribbons, and plaques signifying the earnest desire that everyone win and all have prizes. Everyone trying out for the team makes it; every student is gifted and talented.

There is, however, a catch: If *everyone* is gifted and talented, that's another way of saying that *no one* is gifted or talented. In practice, this means that if everyone can't be on the honor roll, the honor roll is dropped; class rankings are scrapped because no one wants to feel bad; grades are inflated so that everyone can be a straight-A student. "Everyone is special, Dash," says the mom in the movie *The Incredibles.* "Which is another way of saying no one is," Dash mutters.

Indeed, Charles Willie, a professor of education at Harvard, declares that the goal of education should not be "excellence," because that is a matter of personal choice and requires sacrifice. Instead, schools should be concerned with "adequacy."[54]

This aversion to competition is hammered into the mushy skulls of trainee teachers from the moment they enter the swamps of despond and mediocrity that are ed school. A survey by Public Agenda found a dramatic disconnect between the public's expectations of what schools should teach and the beliefs of professors of education—the teachers of teachers. Nearly two-thirds of the ed professors said they thought schools should avoid competition for rewards such as honor rolls, and nearly half supported giving students in team projects a group grade rather than an individual grade.[55] (This is called "collaborative learning," and is otherwise known as "letting the smart kid do all the work.")

Sometimes critics dress up the green toad of jealousy as high principle, and resentment as a passion for "fairness." One educational critic of honor rolls, Mark Mlawer, complained, "Both the educational practice of maintaining an honor roll and the parental practice of public proclamations of this status create and reinforce a certain species of unfairness, one which necessarily causes resentment." Thus, the bumper stickers: MY KID BEAT UP YOUR HONOR STUDENT.[56]

But in the great prestige hierarchy of youth, the honor roll is a relatively minor counterbalance to the genuine honors handed out by nature and by peers—a good jump shot, a body like Lindsay Lohan's, getting elected prom queen, or the ability to beat all the levels of Halo2 in a weekend.

Try as they might, the legions of therapists, social workers, and educationists can't take these advantages away, so they focus instead on the easiest of all: the handful of students who have the ability and have worked hard enough to excel in their school-work. When the honor rolls are dropped, those victories disappear. The burly guys will still get the girls and the fast cars.

Even if the honor student is popular among his peers, the academic honor is still distinctive precisely because it is an *adult* honor that provides the first tangible reward for the values and qualities students will need as grown-ups. Honor rolls say that success in learning math or history, or in developing a new killer-app, is worthy of admiration—a message that students are less likely to receive if left to their peers alone.

But the genuine stupidity in all of this is that at some point you will have to learn how to lose. Because if you don't learn how to fail, life is going to be a very big, very nasty surprise.

Vince Lombardi once said, "The greatest accomplishment is not in never falling, but in rising again after you fall." The edu-nannies believe that it's more important that you fall on something soft and squishy and feel OK about it.

Adults have an advantage here over children because most of them have had the experience of losing and know it is not the end of the world. They know that few defeats are permanent. That's why major-league baseball players handle losses so well, at least in the regular season. There is always tomorrow. Children, whose present seems to fill the entire sky, often don't see that.

On a recent Reality TV show, a young boy whose invention was not accepted by the panel of judges wailed into the camera, "They took away my dream." One of the judges patiently ex-plained to the boy that he was going to be a success, but that he needed to realize that there would be setbacks, that they were part of the process of growing up.

But abolishing the distinction between winning and losing not only takes the sting out of defeat, it also eliminates the in-centives for and the joy of winning.

Defeat doesn't necessarily crush the spirit: sometimes it

inspires. Abraham Lincoln was a notorious loser until he was elected president; the magnitude of the World Series win by the Red Sox is understandable only in the context of their years of futility—a fact that Chicago Cubs fans might keep in mind.

In the 1993 movie *Rudy,* the lead character is Daniel E. "Rudy" Ruettiger, an undersized young man of middling ability, but incredible drive, who sets his sights on making the Notre Dame college football team. Unfortunately for Rudy, his grades aren't good enough to even get him into the university. He enrolls in a community college, where he works to get his grades up, only to meet one setback and frustration after another. But he never gives up. Eventually he is allowed to suit up—and in the movie's climactic scene he is put into the game.

If Notre Dame had had a no-cut policy, if everybody, no matter how untalented, unmotivated, or indifferent, made the squad, Rudy's perseverance and ultimate triumph would have been meaningless.

Some people get this. *The Boston Globe* reports that the practice of giving prizes to everyone has gotten to be so widespread that some schools and sports leagues have actually begun to cut back on the number of trophies. Eventually, someone figured out that if everybody was a winner, nobody really was. "The trophies," explained psychology professor Roy Baumeister, "should go to the winners. Self-esteem does not lead to success in life. *Self-discipline and self-control do. . . .* [Emphasis added]"[57]

RULE 10

Life is actually more like dodgeball than your gym teacher thinks.

It comes at you quickly; it requires alertness and skill; the outcome is unpredictable; the weak can sometimes overcome the strong; it involves elimination and has both winners and losers.

For a while, gym class was one of the last redoubts against rampant kumbayaism. But a decade ago, *The New York Times* reported on the "new gym class," where "competition is out and cooperation is in."[58] Kids no longer got to choose sides, lest anyone be chosen last. Elimination games were frowned upon. Of course, as early-childhood specialist Tom Reed points out, getting singled out and eliminated from competition is part of life. "Life is not always fair," says Reed. But the nannies see it differently.

The most dramatic symbol of the wimpification of childhood has been relentless attack on one of the ultimate tests of the Darwinian concept of the survival of the fittest—a sport that allowed children to take an inflated rubber ball, draw back, take aim, and possibly knock some sense into the educationist nannies running their schools. So far that hasn't happened.

Arguing that violence breeds violence, a student group called Girls Againt Violent Activities (GAVA), in Fairfax, Virginia, successfully pushed for an end to dodgeball in their physical-education class. Schools, they insisted dourly, should not sponsor anything where people are "killed" or "eliminated"—even if it's "just a game."[59]

To the extent that there is such a thing as a phys ed establishment, it joined in the attack. Dodgeball opponents have the full-throated support of the National Association for Sport and Physical Education, a group whose apparent goal is to raise the professional standing of gym teachers by making them as silly as other educationists. The association's executive director, Judith Young, explained, "We take the position that [dodgeball] is not an appropriate instructional activity because it eliminates children and it does not respect the needs of less-skilled children."

"Any time you throw an object at somebody it creates an environment of retaliation and resentment," Thomas Murphy, a physical-education teacher at Tobin Elementary School in Cambridge, Massachusetts, told *The Boston Globe*. "There is nothing positive that can happen except a bully gets to beat up on little kids." Dennis Docheff, of Concordia University's Department of Health and Human Performance, warns of the slippery slope: "In today's world, with so many things breeding violent behavior in children, there is no room for dodgeball anymore."[60] Dodgeball . . . gang membership . . . drive-by shootings . . . the invasion and pillaging of small countries—an almost inevitable progression.

Other critics focused on hurt feelings. "How does elimination from games affect [children's] self-concept and feelings of membership within a group?" worried Robert Kraft of the University of Delaware.[61] (It's unclear if the professor had ever heard of baseball.)

Writing in *The Journal of Physical Education,* Professor Neil Williams of Eastern Connecticut State College consigned dodgeball, along with duck-duck-goose and musical chairs, to the "Physical Education Hall of Shame."[62] These games, according to Professor Williams, encourage "the best to pick on the weak and to be glorified for picking on the weak."

The assault on dodgeball inspired *Sports Illustrated* columnist

Rick Reilly to ask: "You mean there's weak in the world? There's strong? Of course there is, and dodgeball is one of the first opportunities in life to figure out which one you are and how you're going to deal with it." Later in this article Reilly says:

> *I know what all the these NPR-listening, Starbucks-guzzling parents want. They want their Ambers and their Alexanders to grow up in a cozy womb of noncompetition, where everybody shares tofu and Little Red Riding Hood and the big, bad wolf set up a commune. Then their kids will stumble out into the bright light of the real world and find out that, yes, there's weak and there's strong and teams and sides and winning and losing. You'll recognize those kids. They'll be the ones filling up chalupas. Very noncompetitive.*[63]

But the banning of dodgeball wasn't an aberration: it was the tip of a massive—"iceberg" seems somehow inappropriate here—creampuff of wimpification.

RULE 11

After you graduate, you won't be competing against rivals who were raised to be wimps on the playground.

The Duke of Wellington once said that "the Battle of Waterloo was won on the playing fields of Eton"—reflecting his view that competitive sports shape a nation's character. We sure as hell should hope that's not true about America—unless, that is, we plan on going to war against an enemy who also values noncompetitive, risk-free, self-esteem-building play activities for its young.

In Broward County, Florida, school officials banned running on the playground. This would not have been controversial, except that they also banned swings, merry-go-rounds, teeter-totters, crawl tubes, and even sandboxes.[64]

If we can save just one child.

In one California school district, educrats concerned about "bullying, violence, self-esteem and lawsuits" also banned tag, cops-and-robbers, touch football, and every other activity that involved "bodily contact." They apparently meant that quite literally.

"During lunch recess one recent afternoon," reported the *Sacramento Bee* "yard supervisor Janice Hudson spotted a first-grader pushing a girl on the swing."[65]

> *"Do not push," Hudson told the student. "Let her push herself, please."*

"One person can be a little stronger than the other," she said as she walked away.

It's a jungle out there.

One school in Santa Monica, California, announced that it was also banning tag, explaining that "in this game, there is a 'victim' or 'it,' which creates a self-esteem issue."[66]

This is ironic. While kids are sitting around playing Playstation games, or toting Nintendos and Gameboys, and their butts are expanding like mushrooms, professional nannies are hyperventilating about the evils of tag, cops-and-robbers, and most of the other fun stuff that used to take place at recess.

Childhood—or at least the fun part—is falling victim to a potent stew of psychobabble, litigation, and overwrought overprotectiveness. In some schools free play has been replaced by organized relay races and adult-supervised activities in order to protect children from spontaneous outbreaks of creativity. This makes sense to the sort of person who thinks that children must at all costs be protected from the scrapes of life and insulated from the prospect of having to deal with social interactions themselves or having to use their imaginations to make their own kind of play.

Even as playgrounds have become increasingly vanilla, lawsuits have become more common. "You can't swing a dead cat without being sued," said one deputy city attorney—as if anybody would swing any kind of cat, dead or alive, anywhere near a playground these days.[67]

Go out and play in the neighborhood? Build a fort in the woods? Who can risk it?

After all, the nannies have decided that swings and teeter-totters are too dangerous for playgrounds. *USA Today* reports that slides, swing sets, and merry-go-rounds have been replaced "with all-in-one climbing structures that child-development experts say promote both physical fitness and social skills."[68] Much better than fun.

In the past kids did, indeed, fall and scrape their elbows and yes, it is true, broke some bones. These wounds were regarded as badges of growing up, or, at least, of learning to respect the forces of gravity and its interaction with jungle gyms. Playgrounds were once the place where children were taught the nexus between dumb decisions and bad consequences. Now, apparently, they'll have to learn it someplace else, like the freeway.

"Play is one of children's chief vehicles for development," says Joe Frost, an emeritus professor from the University of Texas who runs something called the Play and Playgrounds Research Project. "Right now it looks like we're developing a nation of wimps."[69]

So, if violent games like dodgeball, and other sports with winners and losers, are too threatening to our bubble-wrapped children, what would be acceptable?

How about juggling? Even here, the fragile psyche faces the prospect of dropped balls.

No problem: try juggling scarves.

"The trick," the guru of nonjudgmental scarf juggling says, "is first to teach beginners how to juggle neon-colored scarves. Tennis balls fall quickly and can smash into your face. Scarves are soft and nonthreatening and float down slowly."[70]

Reports the *Los Angeles Times*: "As students throw their scarves into the air, [the teacher] has them repeat the fundamental steps of juggling out loud. As they toss and catch, they chant, 'Toss, catch.' In minutes, they are juggling." Well, actually, they are throwing pieces of cloth into the air, but at least no one is dropping anything and feeling bad about himself.

The possibilities are nearly endless. A teacher described as the "Johnny Appleseed of school juggling" tells teachers they should experiment with extreme versions of scarf tossing—by branching out to discarded socks and dried beans. He reports that one teacher came up with the "nifty substitute" of juggling . . . supermarket produce bags. (Meditate for a moment on the coincidence that obesity, attention-deficit disorder, and extreme sports all began to rise concurrently with the juggling of scarves and grocery bags.)

RULE 12

Humiliation is a part of life. Deal with it.

It is especially a part of adolescent life and is usually administered by peers. The nannies who go to extraordinary lengths to shield children from ever being humiliated or embarrassed don't get the futility of it all. Life is full of embarrassments, from zits to being lousy at basketball to an onset of puberty eighteen months after it was reached by the other guys who sit next to the cheerleaders at lunch. As a way of helping kids cope with the daily trench warfare of adolescence, bubble-wrapping them is useless: you might as well open a cappuccino bar in the midst of the Battle of the Bulge.

So you have a choice: either go into the fetal crouch of embarrassment, or learn to deal with mean kids, unfair cliques, and the fact that some choices lead to bad consequences.

Once in a while, the smaller humiliations can help you learn to avoid the much bigger ones.

In Oklahoma, a mom who was fed up with her fourteen-year-old daughter's lousy grades and bad attitude made her stand on a busy street corner holding a sign that read: "I don't do my homework and I act up in school, so my parents are preparing me for my future. Will work for food.["71]

This tough love, of course, defied every tenet of therapism.

One letter to the editor accused the mother of "killing her daughter psychologically" by embarrassing her publicly. A passing motorist called police to report the alleged incident of self-esteem lowering, and a report on the incident was forwarded to the state Department of Human Services.

The professionals, predictably, inflated themselves into a snit. One professor of child development told reporters that such punishment could do extreme emotional damage. "The trick is to catch them being good," he said. "It sounds like this mother has not had a chance to catch her child being good or is so upset over seeing her be bad, that's where the focus is."

The mom, however, did not subscribe to the catching-them-being-good philosophy and thus proved that she was not as utterly clueless as the professor of child development on the subject of discipline.

"I'm not a professional," said the mom. "But I felt I owed it to my child to at least try." And, in fact, she reported that she had seen a marked improvement in her daughter's behavior in the weeks after the sign incident. Her daughter's attendance at school had been perfect, and her behavior had noticeably improved.

Apparently unaware that she was supposed to be traumatized and emotionally crippled, the girl told reporters that the episode had gotten her attention. "I won't talk back," she said, adding that she hoped to improve her grades enough to be able to play basketball the next year.

Note what the mother in this story did: instead of simply focusing on her daughter's feelings at the moment, she thought ahead to the consequences of her actions for her life as an adult. Instead of concentrating on what her fourteen-year-old thought about her mom this week, she was concerned with what kind of a twenty-three-year-old she would become. She was willing to embarrass her daughter so that she would not have to endure the much longer and deeper embarrassment of living her life as a loser.

RULE 13

You're not going to the NBA, so hold off on the bling and spare us the attitude.

If you are a high school or college athlete, used to being treated like a rock star and having the rules bent for you, here's a reality check: the shoe contract is not in the mail, and you might want to wait on the new Hummer. Also, the get-off-with-a-slap-on-the-wrist card is a temp.

According to the NCAA, less than 3 percent of high school seniors playing on their school's basketball teams will go on to play on an NCAA college team. Fewer than one out of every seventy-five college senior basketball players—about 1.3 percent—will ever be drafted by an NBA team.[72]

So let's run the numbers: you may be the best basketball player at your high school, even the best basketball player in your school's history. But the odds of your making the NBA are only slightly better than your chances of being the first man to land on Venus. Only three out of every ten thousand high school seniors—or about .03 percent—will ever be drafted by the NBA. The other 99.97 percent have to hope they used their skills to get themselves a good education and learn some solid life lessons they can carry over into the real world.*

Unfortunately, this isn't always the case.

---

* The picture's not much brighter for other sports. Only one in five thousand seniors playing girls' high school basketball will ever be drafted by a WNBA team,

In Virginia, some schools considered banning the traditional post-football-game handshake between the opposing teams because some kids failed to properly get into the spirit of the moment.[73] There were reports of kicking, spitting, and various other incidents of unsportsmanlike behavior. This could have been an opportunity for a come-to-Jesus moment when the sweaty athletes were taught the importance of behaving themselves: they could have been made—just for instance—to do some laps or push-ups or ride the bench. Instead, the coaches voted unanimously to ban the handshakes altogether.

"You got beat 56-0 and you want someone to tell you 'Good game' 35 times?" one of the appeasing principals asked. "If you go through the line, there's a possibility that somebody's gonna push somebody, hit somebody, and it's going to be a big problem at the end of the game."

There's a pattern here, because heaven forbid we enforce standards of good conduct and actually teach kids how to behave. Instead of teaching nutrition, schools ban foods (on the assumption that if there are no soda machines in high schools, kids won't be able to find soda anyplace else); instead of teaching critical thinking, schools offer zero tolerance. So, it's hardly surprising that some educators think that asking them to teach sportsmanship is asking too much.

One parent pointed out that the handshake ban seemed to miss the whole point of high school sports.

"None of these kids are pros, but they're going to get jobs somewhere and run up against people who are unfair to them and to others," he wrote. "Scholastic athletics is about how to deal with life and adversity." If you don't learn that in sports, you'll have to pick it up somewhere else.

Play hard, try to excel at your sport, enjoy your teammates and your success—but remember that no matter how good you are, you aren't exempt from the rules that govern other people.

---

and only nine out of ten thousand high school senior football players can look forward to the NFL draft.

RULE 14

Looking like a slut does not empower you.

Fashion statements like low-cut, spaghetti-strapped tops; too-tight, low-riding, midriff-baring, ripped jeans; camisole tops with padded bras; shirts that read, "Who needs a brain when you have these?", send a very specific message to the hormone-rioting males of the species . . . and it is not Respect and Care for Me.

Here's an issue on which open-minded, nonjudgmental sixties liberalism has come full circle, or at least far enough around to bite itself in the butt.

Back then, women fought against being treated as sex objects. Now they find their daughters standing in line to buy T-shirts that say, "Last night I had a nightmare I was a brunette."

Clinical psychologist Patricia Dalton notes, "One young woman pointed out to me, 'It's almost politically incorrect to say that something is inappropriate.' "[74]

So I'll say it, even if your parents won't: you can't go out wearing that skanky T-shirt. And here's a bumper sticker that reads, MEN ARE PIGS: BEHAVE ACCORDINGLY. Keep it with you at all times.

On a recent trip to the ballpark, my fourteen-year-old son and I sat two rows behind a woman who was in her early twenties and about twenty pounds overweight. Whenever she leaned forward, she revealed a large purple-butterfly tattoo on her tailbone along with about two inches of butt crack. One wants to be a gentleman about this sort of thing, but it was not a good look. Plumbers have a long and proud tradition of displaying butt cracks, and unless she was a plumber herself, she was presumably making a conscious fashion statement, and probably was not aware that it was "skank."

When I wondered aloud on my radio show whether young woman who dressed this way knew they were dressing like sluts, one blogger commented:

> *OF COURSE we know what we're doing when we dress ourselves. One obvious way to tell is that if we didn't want to show some skin, we wouldn't accentuate the body parts in question with tattoos and/or piercings. Belly button rings are not worn by girls who always cover up. Neither are those tattoos on the lower back or cleavage (I'll admit to having my own personal tramp stamp on the lower spine location).*
>
> *In general, we know what we're doing when we walk out of the house. We all own mirrors, most of us having a variety of them in many shapes and sizes, to double and triple-check that we know what we're wearing and how we look in it on the way out of the house.*[75]

As one woman put it, "My father used to tell me, 'If it's not for sale, why are you advertising it?' " The girl at the ballpark was advertising a fire sale. What made it even worse was that she was at the ball game with a man I thought was her father. If he was, what was he thinking? If he wasn't . . . well, that's just too easy.

Of course, your generation is not the first to push the limits on what's acceptable to wear; but this may be the first time that the agendas of horny teenage boys, marketers, popular culture, and indecisive parents have all aligned themselves so perfectly. Boys like seminaked girls; the popular culture celebrates skank-chic; marketers fill clothes racks with slutty outfits and even push trainer push-up bras for twelve-year-olds.

And the parents? They're afraid of their children's blogs.

"They don't want a child who complains about them to her friends and the rest of the world on her blog," says Dalton.

Parents, she says, are wishy-washy—unsure of their instincts and often unwilling to assume the rule-making authority of being a grown-up. Above all, they want to be their kids' friends. "They make the mistake of thinking that a good relationship is largely conflict-free."[76]

Apparently, they are less concerned about date rape, sexually transmitted diseases, pregnancy, or what others (including boys and even middle-aged men) might be saying about their daughters on *their* blogs.

The era in which young girls could count on grown-ups to protect them seems to be over; one casualty may be childhood itself, as girls are encouraged to appear to be something they are not. Simply put: letting a twelve-year-old dress like a twenty-one-year-old puts her in harm's way, especially since few girls that young understand what teenage boys are really like. Their fathers, who undoubtedly do remember, are too busy being sensitive, nonjudgmental, and elsewhere.

Writes Dalton:

> *I've polled a number of therapist colleagues, and virtually everyone agreed: We almost never see autocratic, dictatorial parents today; it is far more common to see parents who have relinquished power, and kids who have assumed it. Which makes for very unhappy young people. They are petulant and angry; they lack respect for their parents because their parents haven't inspired respect through real leadership.*[77]

These are also the sort of kids who frequently say, "It's not fair." (See Rule 1.)

RULE 15

Flipping burgers is not beneath your dignity. Your grandparents had a different word for burger flipping. They called it opportunity.

They weren't embarrassed over making minimum wage either. They would have been embarrassed to sit around talking about the contestants on *American Idol* all weekend.

Your grandparents understood that there is dignity in work because it means independence. The reality is that you're not independent until you are paying for your food, rent, clothes, car, gas, insurance, and tuition. And the only way you will be able to do that is to get a job, even a job that might involve getting dirty or smelling like kitchen grease. A job is not degrading. Being a drone or a deadbeat is degrading.

You live in a country with extraordinary opportunity and income mobility; if you start at the bottom, that doesn't mean you will stay there. The important thing to do is to actually *start*, rather than crank up the stereo in your bedroom and lie back while your classmates are asking customers if they want to supersize that.

If you manage to get on the first rung of the work world and to do a good job, you won't stay there for very long. The vast majority of people who were in the lowest 20 percent of earners moved into higher levels in later years. A famous 1995 report by the Federal Reserve Bank of Dallas showed that nearly

three-quarters of people in the bottom fifth of earners in 1975
were in a higher quintile by 1991. That sort of mobility was mir-
rored by a 2000 study by the Economic Policy Institute, which
found that almost 60 percent of people in the lowest quintile in
1969 had moved into a higher quintile by 1996.[78]

How? They worked themselves up. They learned the skills,
attitudes, and habits that helped them climb the economic lad-
der. A lot of people got their start by flipping burgers.

A survey of fast-food workers found that the burger-flipping
jobs had instilled basic employability skills—precisely the skills
that employers complain young people entering the job market
so often lack. The workers learn the importance of being on
time, taking responsibility for mistakes, getting along with others,
taking directions, being well-groomed, and coming to work regularly. Ninety-four percent of workers said they had learned
teamwork; 89 percent said they had learned to deal with customers; 69 percent got a better idea of how a business worked.[79]

Ben Wildavsky writes:

> *A surprising number of burger flippers advance through the
> ranks and enjoy the benefits that go with managerial responsi-
> bility in a demanding business. More important, most employ-
> ees who pass through McDonald's gain the kinds of skills that
> help them get better jobs. Far from sticking its workers in an in-
> escapable rut, McDonald's functions as a de facto job training
> program by teaching the basics of how to work.*[80]

In her book *No Shame in My Game,* Harvard professor Katherine Newman describes the crucial and positive influence that such
jobs had on the lives and attitudes of the working poor in Harlem.
She found that teenagers who worked at fast-food restaurants
formed tightly knit groups of like-minded individuals who clung
tenaciously to their sense of dignity. Newman quotes one four-
year veteran of a restaurant she calls "Burger Barn" defending her
commitment to her job, even in the face of the ridicule of her
peers. "There's a lot more to it than flipping burgers," she says.

"It's a real system of business. That's where I go to see a big corporation at play. Cashiers. The store, how it's run. Production of food, crew workers, service. Things of that nature."[81]

Says Newman: "Older managers help kids understand they have crossed over a dignity line that separates them from ones not working."

While it has become fashionable to deride burger flipping as a dead-end job, Herbert Northup of the Wharton School of Business notes:

> It is perhaps ironic that many of the most insistent advocates of job training programs in this country are the same academics, journalists, and government administrators who condemn fast food jobs as, at best, meaningless dead ends and thus fail to see that the object of their contempt has in effect become one of the most massive, cost-efficient and racially equitable job training programs in our nation's history.[82]

RULE 16

Your parents and your little brother are not as embarrassing as you think. What's embarrassing is ingratitude, rudeness, and sulkiness.

Sulkiness has become the universal performance art of adolescence, even though nobody in the history of mankind has ever looked at a sulky teenager and said, "I'd like to be more like that kid."

The clerk at the fast-food restaurant who thinks that being polite or offering friendly service is somehow beneath him might imagine that his monosyllabic, borderline-rude, sulking nonservice somehow protects his dignity or maybe even expresses his put-upon and wounded self-esteem. It doesn't; there is nothing dignified about acting like a slack-jawed loser (thus the term *slacker*). And the moping-around, moody, hormonal feeling-sorry-for-yourself routine does not make you look like Avril Lavigne; it makes you look like a cliché.

You also need to deal with the fact that being embarrassed is not the worst thing that can happen to you, and certainly not worse than the things that you might be tempted to do to—or not do for—your friends, family, and acquaintances to avoid being embarrassed.

When you look back on it, dumping a friend, going along

with a cruel or irresponsible prank, or avoiding being seen with your grandmother will seem a lot more humiliating than any embarrassment you may have dodged.

RULE 17

Your parents weren't as boring before you were born as they are now. They got that way paying your bills, driving you around, saving for your education, cleaning up your room, and listening to you tell them how idealistic you are.

And by the way, before you save the rain forest from the blood-sucking parasites of your parents' generation, try delousing the closet in your bedroom.

And, yes, it is more than a little ironic to be lectured about the assault on the pristine purity of nature by idealists whose various appendages are tattooed and pierced in ways that nature likely did not intend.

This is what the creators of *South Park* would call a "smug alert": your assumption that because you made dioramas about greenhouse gas emissions, you have a moral leg up on your parents, who actually went to work, saved, invested, and supported their families and now have to spend their most productive years nagging you. This includes asking where you are going and whom you are going with, and other stuff that makes them seem like stuffed shirts from the last century.

If they are annoying you by asking these questions, deal with it. They have to think about what kind of a person you will be when you are twenty-five, or whether you'll even make it to that age. Someday you'll understand and maybe even be a little grateful. If they aren't asking you, someday you'll wonder why they weren't.

As for your superior idealism: nothing is easier than feeling idealistic without actually having to do anything at all. Unfortunately, a bad mood and a desire to piss off your parents are not the same thing as idealism, and they don't save the planet.

"Fretting makes us important," P. J. O'Rourke remarked in *All the Trouble in the World: The Lighter Side of Overpopulation, Famine, Ecological Disaster, Ethnic Hatred, Plague, and Poverty.*

> *Say you're an adult male and you're skipping down the street whistling "Last Train to Clarksville." People will call you a fool. But lean over to the person next to you on a subway and say, "How can you smile while innocents are dying in Tibet?" You'll acquire a reputation for great seriousness and also more room to sit down. . . .*
>
> *And worrying is less work than doing something to fix the worry. This is especially true if we're careful to pick the biggest possible problems to worry about. Everybody wants to save the earth; nobody wants to help Mom do the dishes.*[83]

This is the sort of attitude that explains the protestors who carried signs reading, STOP THE COMMODIFICATION OF WATER at a rally where, O'Rourke noted, "almost everyone was carrying a brand-named bottle of same."[84] Or the kid who wanted to make a bold statement against the corporate world by waving an American flag with all the stars replaced by corporate logos— but who was wearing shoes made by Adidas, and carrying a Mountainsmith backpack and a Swiss army watch. This would be the same demonstration where protestors carried VISUALIZE FUEL-EFFICIENT VEHICLES signs a few yards from the dozens of charter buses hired to carry the idealists to and from the event.[85]

Last year *The New York Times Magazine* ran a cover story[86] asking:

Can a hipster t-shirt be as incendiary as a rock anthem?
Is a cool logo some kind of manifesto?
Does shopping for weird new stuff make you subversive?

The short answer: no.

The same goes for wearing a "Che" T-shirt you bought at the mall: it doesn't make you a revolutionary, or even especially cutting-edge. The guy's been dead for, what, fifty years?

You want cosmic justice? An equitable, fair world, where all wrongs are righted? Where the idle rich pay reparations? Where victims get their just due?

Go out and make enough money to buy your parents a new house.

RULE 18

Life is not divided into semesters. And you don't get summers off.

You don't even get an Easter break. They expect you to show up every day. For eight hours. And you don't get a new life every ten weeks. It just goes on and on.

This really does come as a surprise. I remember a friend I was working with at one of my first jobs as a newspaper reporter. He was about twenty-three years old at the time, and one day he told me that he had a revelation the night before. "I was putting away my albums," he said. "And it suddenly hit me: This is my life. I am living my life. I'm not preparing for my life. I'm not studying for it. This is it." And, of course, he was right.

It's easy to take the seasonal changes for granted. For twelve years or more (depending on how early you started kindergarten), your life changed at the end of every school year; things came to a clean conclusion; there were evaluations and affirmations at the end of each grading period. You got a new teacher and a new set of classmates and, in effect, a new job.

Adult life doesn't work that way. It's measured in years, even decades, not weeks or months; there aren't as many milestones or finish lines; and you don't get merit badges for "stress reduction."

In case this is unclear (and the evidence suggests that it is close to a generational mystery), this means showing up five days a week, at 8:00 a.m. (or whatever the starting time is), and no, you can't take a personal day off because you stayed up till four in the morning watching reruns of *24* or because you were hanging out after the Nelly concert. Until you've put a few years under your belt, this will go on for fifty weeks a year, minus a few holidays. Since the average school year is about 180 days long, this is a considerable upgrade: it means working in June, July, and August . . . maybe even the day after Thanksgiving and Christmas.

And not everything you will have to do will be fun, or even interesting, because your employer doesn't feel the obligation to keep you constantly entertained. This is why it is called work. To get to the more interesting stuff, you might have to prove yourself.

It wouldn't hurt to smile. And lose the tongue piercing.

RULE 19

It's not your parents' fault. If you screw up, you are responsible.

This is the flip side of "It's my life" and "You're not the boss of me" and other eloquent proclamations of your generation. When you turn eighteen, it's on your dime. Don't whine about it, or you'll sound like a baby boomer.

The habit of blaming other people for your problems is easily acquired and difficult to shake. Blaming Mommy and Daddy for your problems is a gateway excuse, and, thanks in part to Sigmund Freud, a sort of starter neurosis for the victim-wannabe class.

Ironically, the baby boomers were the most doted-upon and pampered generation in history—indulged, tolerated, spoiled, and praised with embarrassing frequency. But without a Depression to overcome or a world war to win, they were forced to fall back on pointing fingers at their parents for all of their disappointments and inadequacies.

They not only rebelled against the older generation, they turned the notion of "toxic parenting" into a growth industry, developing theories about "codependency" and turning many of the symptoms of life into a variety of syndromes, disorders, and psychological diseases that could be suffered by just about anybody who didn't get a pony or a Partridge Family poster when he was ten years old. What would daytime television have done without blaming Mommy and Daddy? And would we ever have had a *Ricki Lake Show*?

But adulthood means taking responsibility for your life. Of course, your parents influenced who you are, but from now on the choices are yours, not theirs. If you don't get that, you haven't grown up.

One group that doesn't understand this is the so-called helicopter parents, who have made life so miserable for college officials in recent years. The name derives from their insistence on hovering over their grown children, monitoring, micromanaging, and second-guessing their choices of everything from dorm rooms to courses. On some campuses the infestation of helicopter parents has gotten so bad that the school authorities have had to develop special programs simply to distract them.

By definition, the helicopter parents are admitting failure.

They send their children into an environment packed with counselors, guidance officers, and housing assistants, yet they are convinced that their children will flounder outside of the stress-free familial bubble in which they have spent the last eighteen years. Instead of preparing their children for the vicissitudes and trials of real life, the overprotective helicopter parents hang on in even the most accepting, structured college environments.[87] Of course, there are frustrations, bureaucratic screwups, bad course choices, and awful roommates. They are among the first—quite mild—reality checks for young people.

"Middle-class parents especially assume that if kids start getting into difficulty they need to rush in and do it for them, rather than let them flounder a bit and learn from it," notes historian Peter Stearns. "I don't mean we should abandon them," he says, "but give them more credit for figuring things out."[88]

If you can't handle dealing with your Resident Assistant or class schedule, then obviously your parents didn't actually raise you. You didn't grow up. Responsible parents prepare their children for navigating life on their own. By definition, helicopter parents haven't done so. David Anderegg, professor of psychology at Bennington College, has to deal with the new breed of hyperattentive parents, who think they have to make every possible decision for their children.

"If you have an infant and the baby has gas, burping the baby is being a good parent," says Anderegg. "But when you have a ten-year-old who has metaphoric gas, you don't have to burp him. You have to let him sit with it, try to figure out what to do about it. He then learns to tolerate moderate amounts of difficulty, and it's not the end of the world."[89]

Cell phones have made the problem even worse. In the hands of helicopter parents and their anxious offspring, says Harg Estroff Marano, the cell phone has become the "eternal umbilicus"—the high-tech umbilical cord that keeps young people "in a permanent state of dependency."[90]

In the past, young people were raised to internalize the values of their parents and then learn how to apply those values to real-life situations and choices. But, says Anderegg, "cell phones keep kids from figuring out what to do. They've never internalized any images; all they've internalized is 'call Mom or Dad.'"[91]

Businesses now are reporting that helicopter parents are showing up in the workplace, calling on behalf of their adult (the word is used here in the narrowest sense) children, even showing up with them at job interviews. Some managers have taken to calling such parents "the kamikaze parents." They have already terrorized guidance counselors, harassed admissions officers, and browbeaten clerks at Starbucks who made disappointing lattes.

"It's unbelievable to me that a parent of a 22-year-old is calling on their behalf," one manager told *The Wall Street Journal.* Other managers relate tales of interviewees who tell prospective employers, "Let me talk to my parents. I'll get back to you."[92]

In fact, the message the super helicopter parents are sending is this: "You shouldn't trust my child's judgment, because I obviously don't." While they might think they are simply being supportive, they are acknowledging that at no time in the last twenty, twenty-one, or twenty-two years did they ever succeed in raising independent, self-sufficient adults who could deal with life's issues on their own.

RULE 20

Smoking does not make you look cool. . . . It makes you look moronic.

Next time you're out cruising, watch an eleven-year-old with a butt in his mouth. That's what you look like to anyone over twenty when you are smoking.

You may also be under the impression that smoking makes you thinner and sexier. Maybe it does, but consider the trade-off: yellow teeth, stained fingers, breath like an ashtray, prematurely winkled skin, charcoal lungs, and eventual heart disease. And not many people can pull off looking hot while they are breathing through a tube.

You also don't establish your individual identity by having the same nose ring as everyone else, or by wearing the same clothes, listening to the same music, and having the same ideas about politics. This is called conformity. Also—trust me on this—the tattoos won't look so good when you're fifty. Actually a lot of things that might seem like good ideas now . . . aren't.

RULE 20B

Even though you have a cool mom, a wimpy principal, and a spineless school board, the world does not revolve around you or your need to express yourself with a nose ring.

This is a true story: A fourteen-year-old girl nags her mother for permission to get her nose pierced. At first the mom resists. Her daughter, after all, is a bit young to start getting things pierced or tattooed. But her daughter begs, cajoles, wheedles, and bargains, and finally Mom—who undoubtedly wants to be her girl's best friend—gives in.

Unfortunately, the nose piercing is more than a bad adolescent fashion choice. In this girl's state, it is illegal for anyone under the age of sixteen to get anything other than ears pierced; it is also against school rules. When school officials point out the rules, the girl refuses to remove her newly acquired nose stud. She defies her middle school principal and is given a five-day in-house suspension.

Accustomed by now to adults caving in and to getting her way, the girl appeals on behalf of her nose-piercing self-expression to the full school board, which takes the opportunity to . . . fawn over her.

"It takes a lot of courage for an adult to stand up for what they believe in," the board president told the fourteen-year-old, thus demonstrating her own lack of courage to enforce the district's rules. "And I think I speak for the entire board by saying that I think we're proud of you."[93] If there were gagging sounds from the audience, they were not recorded.

Understandably inflated by the experience, the defiant girl explained: "I feel it is important to express yourself in an open environment, such as a school. I was always taught by my teachers, peers and parents that school is a place to find out who you are and where you stand. I am simply doing what I was taught."

And indeed she was, this product of self-affirming, self-expressing, therapeutic education. Clearly, she had not been taught to have any respect for authority. She was unaccustomed to thinking that the word *no* would ever apply to her directly. Nor was she taught that there are occasions when she may not be able to have everything she wants. Or that she may have to defer gratification, say, until she comes of legal age.

Apparently, if she is ever to learn those lessons, someone will have to buy her this book.

RULE 21

You're offended? So what? No, really. So what?

A willingness to be offended at the smallest slight is not a sign of a superior consciousness—it is a decision to be a whiner and an emotional bully.

This may come as a surprise, but living in a free country does not mean that you are free from annoyance or immune to things that offend you, and it certainly does not give you a license to silence, reeducate, or harass people with whom you disagree. If you want to avoid being offended, you should probably try a Buddhist monastery rather than, say, public transportation or a modern university.

Almost everybody can play the "I am offended" card: minorities, majorities, women, men, liberals, conservatives, gays, lesbians, straights, Catholics, Muslims, Native Americans, Hispanics, African Americans, feminists, evangelicals, blondes, short people, fat people, thin people, lawyers, and guys who are going bald.

The tyranny of the easily offended is exercised by the sort of people who walk around with sensitivities locked, loaded, and holstered in easy reach in case they encounter the slightest glimmer of sexism, racism, classism, heightism, lookism, or fattism or even excessive amounts of cologne. And they usually find what they're expecting. In a previous book (*A Nation of Victims*), I noted that America is increasingly crisscrossed by invisible trip wires of emotional, racial, sexual, and psychological grievance.

Witches are offended by Halloween; multiculturalists are offended by school nicknames and books by dead white guys; feminists are offended by mascara and guys who open doors for
women. Atheists are offended by public prayer; believers are offended by the objections of atheists; and agnostics don't know
what to believe, so they pretty much stay out of it. Almost everybody, including Scientologists, is offended by *South Park*. And
don't even get me started on Christmas, which has become a
veritable riot of hyperoffended finger-pointing, pitting people
offended by carols, crèches, and Christmas trees against militants
who are offended by people who say, "Happy holidays" instead
of "Merry Christmas."

Even offhand remarks, or the inadvertent use of the wrong
word, can stir the machinery of offense into action. The loudest
complaints often come from advocates who claim to be empowering the victims of the slur. After the 2006 Masters Tournament, Tiger Woods remarked, "I putted atrociously today. Once I
got on the greens, I was a spaz."[94] Hypersensitive advocates for
people with cerebral palsy declared themselves offended, and
Woods was compelled to apologize on his Web site. But was anybody *really* offended? And was anybody really empowered?

At one time, people lived by the saying "Sticks and stones
may break my bones, but words can never hurt me." Sure it was
simplistic, but it told us not to let the words of others determine
our sense of self-worth.

In contrast, the permanently offended want you to react to
words the same way you would react to a brick thrown in your
face; they assume that "victims" are so feeble that their self-
image will be crushed by a word—even if no offense whatso-
ever was intended.

In any case, the search for inoffensiveness is often frustrating
and futile. As attorney and commentator Rick Esenberg has noted,
"Trying to find a set of nonoffensive words for characteristics that
truly are a disadvantage is a game with no end."[95] A list of the "10
worst words" in Britain, for example, includes such obviously in-
sulting terms as "retard" and "window-licker," but also terms like

"special," "brave," and even "wheelchair-bound," a phrase presumably used to refer to people who are . . . wheelchair-bound.[96] Since terms like *brave* and *special* were introduced at one time as inoffensive euphemisms, this is tail chasing with a vengeance.

Of course, the real irony in the kerfuffle over Wood's use of the term *spaz* was that he plays a game (golf) that has since time immemorial rated the skill of players using the term *handicap*.

The lesson here is that if you wake up every day looking for something to be offended by, you'll find it. My advice: Get over it. Get used to the fact that other people will bother, annoy, aggravate, exasperate, and irritate you. You will run into words, gestures, and pictures you don't like. But so what? You don't live in Mr. Rogers' neighborhood anymore.

There is another reason to avoid being offended all the time: It's exhausting.

Keeping up with all the resentments is draining; it's hard being indignant 24/7. If you invite the easily offended to hang out in your head, they'll take up space, won't clean up after themselves, and will eat all the chips. So why let them in?

RULE 22

You are not a victim. So stop whining.

On any given day, something like 84 percent of the American public could, if they wished, claim they are victims of something or other and could complain, wheedle, and demand that somebody do something about it.

This shouldn't be a surprise, because there are obvious benefits to being a victim. First of all, it's relatively easy: being a victim means never having to say you're sorry. Victims aren't responsible, because there's always somebody else to blame. Victimhood also provides a certain moral superiority, a sort of all-purpose trump card in debates, and a handy source of political power. But there's a downside as well: people whose identity is defined by their victimhood often find that they are trapped by it since if they take responsibility for their failings, they run the risk of losing their victim status. And then where are they? Better not to start in the first place.

Try this exercise:

In the blank, fill in the worst thing that ever happened to you:_____.

On a list of the top thousand genuine victims, you wouldn't make the list of alternates:

The Jewish victims of Kristallnacht; American victims of the Bataan Death March; the Japanese who were interned in camps in this country during World War II; victims of the Holocaust;

women who lived under the Taliban; Armenians massacred by the Turks; Muslims murdered by Serbs; the slaves who built the pyramids; Aztec human sacrifices; Ukrainian peasants starved by Stalin; victims of Saddam Hussein's "rape rooms"; American Indians who were driven off their land; virgins sacrificed to pagan gods; victims of the atomic bomb dropped on Hiroshima, or the firebombing of Dresden; or Christian martyrs who were barbecued to death.

No matter how bad your gym teacher is or how mean your parents are, you haven't been jailed, beaten, tortured, exiled, crucified, whipped, drawn and quartered, tarred and feathered, or shot for your religious or political opinions. You haven't been left to die on an exposed mountain, enslaved in the cargo holds of traders' ships, or starved in the Irish potato famine. Your house wasn't seized to quarter foreign troops; you haven't been raped by roaming Mongol hordes; your family hasn't been seized by warring Somali warlords; you haven't been imprisoned for reading forbidden books or locked inside a burning school because authorities wouldn't let you leave without wearing the proper head-covering. You haven't had your clitoris removed as women in sub-Saharan Africa have; you were never forced into the British navy where sailors got scurvy and had their teeth fall out; you didn't get trench foot in no-man's-land or have to go over the top at Gallipoli. You've never been forced to sit through Wagner's Ring Cycle or compelled to see a movie starring Paris Hilton.

The odds are that you have most of your original limbs, and have been spared most disfiguring diseases. You probably do not have cholera, the Ebola virus, or AIDS. You are unlikely to die of polio or tuberculosis. You did not grow up during a famine, drought, or locust infestation. It's unlikely you ever went to bed hungry because your parents could not afford a hunk of bread (though you may have done so because of your latest trendy diet or eating disorder).

Confronted with complaints that modern American

women are victims of oppressive male-dominated culture, author Edward Abbey responded in his novel *The Fool's Progress:*

> *Tell it to the Marines. Tell it to those grunts, all boys, who sweated, fought, suffered, and died in the green hell of Vietnam. . . . Tell it to the serfs of merrie olde England who plowed, sowed, reaped, and saw the fruits of their labor stolen from them by the lords—and ladies—who claimed ownership of the land. . . . Tell it to . . . the slaves of the Deep South. . . . Tell it to those who died in the Coliseum, to Spartacus and the twenty thousand slaves, all men, who were crucified with him by the victorious Romans. Tell it to the slaves—men, women, and children—who built the Pyramids, the Great Wall of China, the Parthenon, the Apian viaducts, the walls of Toledo and temples of Mexico, the lost and forgotten horrors of imperial Africa. . . . Tell it to Aleksandr I. Solzhenitsyn and the surviving zeks of the Gulag and the KGB. . . ."*[97]

In other words: Get a grip. It's not as bad as you think.

Once, when I was tempted to feel sorry for myself because I had just lost my job, my father put things in perspective by asking me, "Will you have a refrigerator?" When I told him that of course I would have a refrigerator, he said, "Well then, how bad can it really be?" I wasn't a victim.

RULE 23

Someday you will have to grow up and actually move out of your parents' house.

Previous generations crossed the frozen Bering Strait, rounded the Cape of Good Hope, discovered the New World, traveled the Oregon Trail, climbed Mount Everest, plunged into the rain forests of South America, explored the Great Barrier Reef, journeyed to the South Pole, and landed on the moon.

So far, though, the great pioneering move of Generation Me is back home to live with Mom.

There are a lot of creative euphemisms for people who fail to launch: *emerging adults, theshholders, twixters,* and *kidults.* None of them should be taken as compliments.

They all reflect the fact that a generation that nobody prepared for the real adult world is—not surprisingly—refusing to grow up, sometimes delaying adulthood into their late twenties or even into their thirties. The number of so-called boomerangs—adult children between the ages of eighteen and thirty-four who move back home—is up by 50 percent since 1970.[98] According to the census, 56 percent of men and 43 percent of "adults" between the ages of eighteen and twenty-four continue to live with one or more parent. Even more continue to rely on their parents' checkbooks well past the age when grown-ups were once expected to pay their own way.[99]

But however long you hang out at your parents' house, sooner or later it will come to an end. Eventually, you'll have to move your stuff out and make your own bed.

It used to be that kids couldn't wait to get out of the house, get their own place, and experience the freedom and pride of self-sufficiency and self-reliance. But that has changed: for several years now, social scientists have tried to figure out why young people are delaying adulthood.

So many young people are lingering in this netherworld between adolescence and independence that demographers have had to change the definition of adulthood itself. Writing in a publication of the American Sociological Association in 2004, a team of social scientists studying the lengthening road to adulthood concluded that "it takes much longer to make the transition to adulthood today than decades ago, and arguably longer than it has at any time in America's history."[100]

Comparing census numbers from 1960 and 2000, the social scientists found a dramatic decline in the percentage of young adults who, by age twenty or thirty, "have completed all of the traditionally-defined major adult transitions (leaving home, finishing school, becoming financially independent, getting married and having a child)." Back in 1960, 77 percent of women and 65 percent of men had completed all five transitions to adult life by age thirty. By 2000, that figure had dropped to 46 percent of women and less than a third (31 percent) of men.

If researchers looked at a "more contemporary definition of adulthood"—leaving out marriage and kids—the numbers were less dramatic, but still substantial. The percentage of thirty-year-old men who had left home, were financially independent, and had completed their schooling was twelve points lower than the percentage for their counterparts in 1960. The percentage of women who were independent by the time they turned thirty was down by ten points.

The sociologists concluded that "American society will have to revise upward the 'normal' age of full adulthood, and develop ways to assist young people through the ever-lengthening transition."[101]

That's obviously one option. The other is to recognize that when grown-ups refuse to grow up something has gone terribly wrong and that maybe we should question the way we prepare our children for the adult world.

Occasionally, observers blame this prolonged adolescence on the economy, because it is supposedly so much tougher these days to get through school and get started in a career. Right. Tell it to the guys who kicked Hitler's butt and used the GI Bill to get their college degrees. Somehow they managed to grow up. So did their parents, and they not only didn't have cable television, they were probably lucky to have their own bedroom and indoor plumbing. But they grew up, and if they did live with their parents, they were probably helping to support the oldsters—not the other way around.

So the economic excuse is just that—an excuse, and a pretty lame one too. The kidults aren't hanging around the house and letting Mom do the laundry because times are so tough; they are there because times are so easy. Home is where nobody makes any demands; and if you've been raised in bubble wrap, why would you want to leave it just because you've reached the age of majority and they let you vote?

Seriously, given their entitled lifestyles, why should they actually fly the nest? If they ever went out on their own, how could they expect to be able to drive as nice a car as they had in high school? Who would make their breakfasts? Fold their socks? Do their dishes?

One of the role models for the refuse-to-grow-up generation is a twenty-nine-year-old college student named Johnny Lechner, who has parlayed his thirteen-year-long stay in school into a sort of celebrity as King of the Slackers. He's been written up nationally, appeared on ABC-TV's *Good Morning America, The Late Show with David Letterman,* and *Inside Edition,* and has cut endorsement deals with an energy-drink company and *National Lampoon.*

"His bedroom wall," reports the *Milwaukee Journal Sentinel,* "is covered with photos of fraternity parties, Halloween celebrations and spring break romps."[102] Lechner's endless stay in school inspired the University of Wisconsin Board of Regents to adopt a rule that doubles full-time tuition for students who exceed 165 credits, or amass 30 more credits than their degree requires. By the end of the 2005–2006 school year, Lechner had amassed around 250 credits, so the slacker tax is widely dubbed "the Johnny Lechner Rule" throughout the university.

Lechner not only offers no apologies, he's actually proud of his status: "I have 18-, 19- and 20-year-old girls throwing themselves at me in bars." Notes the newspaper: "It's not just the girls. Grocery store clerks recognize his name. He has a following of older male students on campus who seek to emulate him."

A celebrity among grocery clerks. Can it get any better than that? Maybe not. Johnny Lechner may have peaked, and that's the problem.

Many students apparently regard the aging Lechner as a loser, and patience with his schtick is running thin. A twenty-six-year-old slacker can be charming; a thirty-something undergrad who hangs out at parties is borderline creepy. "It's getting old," says the editor of the student newspaper. "For the sanity of the rest of the campus, we want him to get out of here."

On some level Lechner gets this: he has a Web site, lots of publicity every time he fails to graduate, and his God-like status among grocery-store employees. In other words, he knows he has found his niche. Once he graduates, it all ends—he loses his edge and his angle: he's just another aging loser who hasn't managed to acquire any special skills and whose only accomplishment is a failure to get on with his life.

At least he has a lot of company. J. T. O'Donnell, a Generation Y career coach, says Lechner's failure to grow up has become so widespread, she's given it a name: "On-Set Career Crisis." This syndrome seems to afflict an awful lot of the spoiled, entitled, privileged kids whose expectations make the transition to being on their own so traumatic.[103]

"The on-demand, instant-gratification generation has been coaxed into desired behaviors using all sorts of bribes," she says.

"Presents, praise, stickers, grades; you name it, this generation is used to being given an incentive to do what's expected of them."

So what's the incentive to grow up, get a job, and move out, other than having someone kick you in the pants if you don't?

How about avoiding the disgrace of living in your childhood bedroom at age thirty-five and being regarded as an aging loser and a pathetic momma's boy? That's not incentive enough?

In any case, moving home only postpones the inevitable: Adulthood and responsibility are lurking out there, biding their time. You can slack, but you can't hide forever.

RULE 24

Batman's girlfriend is right: "It's not who you are un-
derneath, but what you do that defines you."*

Good intentions aren't enough; it's not enough to be
"sincere"—you have to make the right choices and do the right
thing.

Every jerk thinks that deep down inside he's a good person, and
the jails are full of the misunderstood. Criminologist Anthony
Daniels notes that most criminals believe in what he calls the
"Real Me," who isn't the guy who beats people up, commits
robberies or rapes, or deals drugs. "No, the 'Real Me' is an im-
maculate conception, untouched by human conduct; it is the
unassailable core of virtue that enables me to retain my self-
respect whatever I do."[104]

People who think that they should be judged by their feeling
usually appeal to the sincerity of their intentions. But sincerity
only takes you so far. It's not enough for a surgeon or an architect
to be sincere; the one also has to perform surgeries in such a way
that patients survive, and the other has to construct buildings that
won't fall down. Sincerity alone won't save a heart patient or feed
the sick at a soup kitchen. Writer Tom McMahon notes that our
intentions are tested by life's tougher situations.

---

* From *Batman Begins*.

Love takes care of you when you are sick. It visits you in the hospital. It comes to the funeral when your loved one dies. Love doesn't forget to call. It doesn't forget to visit. Because love always *acts the part. It doesn't act some other part.*

If someone says, "I'm sorry I never visited you when you were in the hospital for 6 months, but I still love you," you know it's not true, because that's not how love would act. The not-coming-by-for-6-months is a different part, one that love doesn't act.[105]

In other words, love is a *behavior,* not just a *feeling.* It doesn't matter if you are *sincere.* It matters what you *do.*

RULE 25

Pi does not care what you think.

Regardless of your opinion, personal preferences, or need to be "true to yourself," pi, the ratio of the circumference of a circle to its diameter, is approximately 3.14159265358979323846. This isn't like the debate about red versus purple pens: pi is what it is, no matter how you feel about it.

Water boils at 212 degrees Fahrenheit (100 degrees centigrade); the speed of light in a vacuum is 186,282 miles per second; a basketball court is ninety-four feet long; the diameter of a basketball rim is eighteen inches; and the peak of Mount Everest is 29,035 feet above sea level.

Science-fiction writer Philip K. Dick defines reality as that which "when you stop believing in it, doesn't go away."[106] In other words, not all truth is subjective or relative, despite the number of times you hear the phrase "Well, that's just my opinion." Of course, some things *are* genuinely matters of personal opinion, like your taste in music, or whether you like red more than blue. But other facts stubbornly refuse to accommodate themselves to your needs, desires, intentions, or feelings. Remember that, the next time you are tempted to think that the world revolves around you.

Engineers can pursue their bliss, but if they don't know the mechanical properties of steel, their buildings will fall down; and even if they have been protected from dodgeball their whole lives, lawyers have to know the rules of procedure or see their briefs tossed out of court. Your personal views have little bearing on the physics of a two-and-a-half-ton car smashing into a light pole.

One day, when he wasn't managing the Civil War, Abraham Lincoln said: "How many legs does a dog have if you call the tail a leg? Four. Calling a tail a leg doesn't make it a leg." As Michael Barone might put it, Hard America recognizes this; Soft America doesn't.[107]

Like a softball team that wanders into the New York Yankees' spring training camp, the educrats, counselors, professors, pundits, and therapists of Soft America often regard Hard America with a mixture of disdain and anxiety. People who talk or emote for a living always have a nagging inferiority complex about people who *do* things, especially those who have to do things that can be measured and that can have exacting standards of excellence. Surgeons, firefighters, pilots, and architects have to get it right; Soft America just needs to feel OK about it.

RULE 26

A moral compass does not come as standard equipment.

People do not always naturally know right from wrong, and your feelings are no more a reliable guide to moral and ethical conduct than your appetite is a guide to advanced algebra.

H. L. Mencken once described conscience as "the mother-in-law whose visit never ends."[108] That assumes that you have a mother-in-law and that you have a conscience, or at least one that is informed enough to know the difference between right and wrong.

Unfortunately, you may not have been taught the difference, since nonjudgmentalism is nearly a sacred principle in society today. Instead of giving children ethical handholds, we encourage them to "discover" their own values—an approach based on the rather fantastic notion that since none of the civilizations anywhere in the world throughout the entire sweep of human history has been able to work out a moral code of conduct worthy of being passed on, we can leave it to seventh-graders to work one out on their own.

This reduces moral choices to a matter of personal taste, like picking a red sweater instead of a blue one. If there is no right or wrong answer, nobody's choice is any better than anyone else's. Nonjudgmentalism is convenient and easy, but it isn't moral reasoning: it just means we can rationalize any choice we make. And most of us are very, very good at rationalizing.

That seems to explain a new study of twenty-five thousand high school students, which found disturbingly high levels of cheating, theft, and dishonesty—but also found that the same kids felt good about their ethics, character, and trustworthiness.[109]

The survey by the Josephson Institute of Ethics found that nearly two-thirds (62 percent) of high school students admitted that they had cheated on exams, while more than one in four (27 percent) had stolen from a store within the previous twelve months. Forty percent said they "sometimes lie to save money."

But somebody's also been handing out gold stars for ethical self-esteem: Almost all of the students (98 percent) said that it was important for them to be a person of good character, but despite acknowledging that they lied and cheated, 92 percent said they were satisfied with their ethics and character. Nearly three-quarters (74 percent) of the students rated their own ethics higher than those of their peers.

"Still," remarked Institute president Michael Josephson, "it can't be comforting to know that the majority of the next generation of police officers, politicians, accountants, lawyers, doctors, nuclear inspectors and journalists are entering the workforce as unrepentant cheaters."

The Josephson Institute attributed the disconnect between the dishonesty and the smug self-satisfaction of the students to "high levels of cynicism," especially among young men.

Two-thirds of boys said, "In the real world, successful people do what they have to do to win, even if others consider it cheating." More than half (52 percent) of the girls agreed.

So here's the reality check: In the real world cheating and lying can destroy your reputation, and throw your career, your life, and your future into the crapper. It can cost you your family, your home, your job, even your freedom. You can talk to all the "helping" professionals you want, but ultimately you are going to be judged on whether or not you can be trusted.

BONUS RULE

"Garbage in, garbage out" applies to what you listen to and watch just as much as it does to what you eat.

There's something ironic about the number of people who are careful to put only low-fat, sugar-free, vegan, whole-grain, organic food into their mouths and who then turn around and pump raw sewage into their heads.

Whether it is violent video games that glorify mass murder or rap music filled with references to "bitches" and "hos," a steady diet of depression, gloom, and violence will eventually have an effect on your brain cells. You might as well stick your head into a toxic-waste dump as fill it with the hate and despair of much of popular culture.

RULE 27

Your sexual organs were not meant to engage in higher-order thinking or decision making.

You knew this, didn't you? Except you still listen to them as if they made sense, and if you are a sixteen-year-old boy, you are probably listening to them . . . all . . . the . . . time.

There's a reason for this: adults are reluctant to bring this up, and maybe some of them have forgotten, but sex is fun. It feels very, very good, and unless you live in Upper Mongolia, you are being inundated with messages pushing you to hook up and get your groove on.

Cheerleading for the glamorous and active sex life, popular culture has given your Wild Willie a megaphone, a billboard, a network, and about a thousand Web sites. Turn on MTV, click through prime-time television, or open any popular magazine, and you'll get the impression the entire world is in heat. Pull into a convenience store, and you might run into a display for "Horniest Goat Weed: sex stimulant pill for men and women."[110] Go online, and you'll find ten thousand porn sites where people do things your grandparents didn't even think were anatomically possible. And it is all completely sincere: your sexual organs sincerely want what they want, and they want it now.

To resist all of this requires a considerable amount of something you might not have been taught: self-control.

A study of children by the London School of Economics found 57 percent of nine-to-nineteen-year-olds who go online at least once a week run across pornography. (Parents are clueless: only 16 percent think their children have seen porn online.)[111]

A generation ago, the average boy used to sneak his father's *Playboy* magazines into the bedroom to take a ride on the wild side of the hormonal tornado. Hugh Hefner's fantasies did the trick for Dad, but the average video on MTV would have put him into cardiac arrest. To be sure, hormones rioted in the ancient days of your parents' youth, but there were limits. Even in the legendary Summer of Love, most guys went to bed alone and frustrated, which is why so many baby boomers are haunted by the thought that they missed out on something. For a lot of them, Viagra makes up for the disappointments of the sixties and seventies.

For generations, guys tried a variety of lines on young women, including eloquent pleas to let them show their love and "This is my last night before D-day," but girls often drew the line, and results were mixed. A few guys even tried to convince girlfriends that oral sex wasn't really sex, but nobody ever bought it until Bill Clinton came along. Your parents would probably be shocked by the whole idea of "friends with benefits."

Some studies suggest that one out of every three girls has had sex by the time she is sixteen; two-thirds have had sex by the time they are eighteen, about the same ratio as boys, although boys are more likely to lie about it. In other words, a generation that seldom heard any grown-up tell them no is having a hard time saying no to one another, even though the consequences are often brutal.

Pundits with pretensions to seriousness like to say that poverty leads to teenage pregnancy. But this, of course, is absurd: teenage pregnancy is caused by horny teenagers. It takes a special kind of journalist–policy wonk to think that economics trump hormones.

But it is true that one of the best ways to become poor is to get pregnant. Girls who get pregnant as teens are more likely to drop out of school, to not attend college, and to end up on some sort of welfare. And that's just for starters.

Young people who begin having sex at an early age are more likely to get sexually transmitted diseases (STDs) or to become depressed, and are even more likely to attempt suicide. Their babies tend to have lower birth weights and to do badly in school, and statistically are more likely to be abused and neglected. According to one study, the sons of teen moms are 13 percent more likely to end up behind bars. Daughters of teen moms are 22 percent more likely to become teen mothers themselves—a good argument for condoms, but an even better one for holding off, unless of course you like playing Russian roulette with your future.[112]

Delaying gratification requires not merely self-control but a willingness to respect yourself and your partner—a good habit to get into before you try to sort out the whites from the red underwear together at the neighborhood Laundromat.

A corollary rule here: self-control + trust + dependability = freedom. "Being yourself" does not mean that you have to be a slave to "I want." You don't liberate yourself from your parents or teachers by being unable to control your moods, angers, hungers, or lusts. In the past, most thoughtful grown-ups cautioned young people against being dominated by their passions and letting emotions run wild. The process of civilization could even be defined as teaching the art of self-control. This art is not necessarily the same thing as "following your bliss," which often appears in the guise of a tight pair of jeans.

In the meantime, by all means, do whatever you like with a consenting adult in the privacy of your own bedroom, provided that you are also an adult, are married to the other consenting adult, are paying for the bedroom, are using protection, are up-to-date on all the latest information on STDs, have health insurance that covers OB-GYN and pediatric services, and understand how child support works. Otherwise, keep your Wild Willie parked.

RULE 28

Somebody may be watching. . . .

Every time you log onto the Internet, including sites like My Space and Facebook, you should think about the movie archvillain who sneers, *"You have no idea who you are dealing with."* On the net that is literally true.

When you post something on the World Wide Web, you have no idea who might be reading or seeing it, and you have absolutely no control over how it will be used. Brag about your weekend of bingeing and hooking up on My Space, and chances are that the prospective employer who will be interviewing you on Monday is adding this juicy information to your file. (Don't count on the job.) When you post your picture, or rate the junior girls as "hot or not," the posting could be downloaded by classmates, a neighbor, a sexual predator, or an assistant principal. You might even get a call from the father of a girl whose legs you said were fat. Don't say you weren't warned.

This is also a very good argument for never doing anything in front of a Web-cam that you wouldn't do onstage at a school assembly.

"Conscience," H.L. Mencken once observed, "is that inner voice that warns us that somebody is looking."

What if everybody were looking? If you are not sure about getting a moral compass, try this: when you are deciding whether to do something, imagine how you will look on the front page of the newspaper. (For purposes of this chapter, let's assume that people still actually read newspapers, but if that seems too old-fashioned, feel free to substitute *Inside Edition, The Daily Show,* or a particularly juicy posting on the Internet.)

You will embarrass not just yourself, but also everyone else who has an investment in you, starting with your parents. Whether it is driving drunk or cheating on a test, lighting up a joint in the backseat of your buddy's car, calling a stripper for the frat party, fudging your taxes, or participating in a hazing ceremony involving underwear, blindfolds, and cell-phone cameras—things look different in the morning and a lot different in black-and-white, or live on videotape at eleven o'clock.

In a zero-tolerance world, private slips can become public scandals, and you can't count on people in authority to cut you any slack. So when you are making your choices, ask yourself. How would this look to other people? How would I explain it to my parents? My brothers and sisters? My friends? My classmates? My coach? My colleagues? My neighbors? My girlfriend/boyfriend? Or people I just meet in the Laundromat?

Would you be able to explain it in a way that would make them all see it your way? Would they get the joke? Or would they wonder what you could *possibly* have been thinking?

Of course, at the time, they all thought they had a good idea:

> *The high school students who put laxative in their teacher's coffee and now face criminal charges.*

> *The members of the girls' soccer team whose underwear initiation is on every cable channel.*

> *The high school basketball team captain who will miss the state tournament because someone posted on the Internet a picture of him chugging a beer.*

> *The ex-valedictorian who posted obscene photoshopped pictures of school staffers on MySpace.*

The firefighter who's been arrested for having child porn on his computer.

The NFL player who has to explain (starting with his wife, then the parents, then police) why he was in the hot tub with teenage girls from a local Catholic high school.

The lawyer who "borrowed" the funds he was supposed to keep in trust for one of his clients.

The CEO who has to explain how $200,000 of his company's funds got spent on his birthday party.

Occasionally, you will encounter someone who will tell you that we shouldn't care about what other people think. But unless you plan to live in a remote desert hermitage, this is nonsense.

What makes all of this even scarier is that modern technology has created the "permanent record" that teachers have been using for generations to scare kids. Except, now it really is permanent, and all you have to do is Google it.

RULE 29

Learn to deal with hypocrisy.

Your parents may have smoked dope, fooled around, and done a lot of the things they tell you not to do. That's not a license to ignore them: sometimes when we are young and dumb, we grow up and don't want the people we love to do dumb things too.

"Hypocrisy," observed François, Duc de La Rochefoucauld, "is the tribute that vice pays to virtue."[113] (He would have known, of course, being French.)

What he meant was that hypocrisy doesn't discredit virtue; it simply admits that it has nicer clothes, so it borrows them. A hypocrite is someone who says one thing, does another, but at least knows that he should sound like he is doing the right thing. In other words, his hypocrisy acknowledges that there is a right thing and that it is preferable to what he is doing.

Usually, the hypocrite is easily spotted: the priest who preaches chastity but also molests choirboys; the celebrity who flies around the country in a Gulfstream jet but also nags soccer moms in minivans about energy conservation; members of Congress discussing ethics.

But is it hypocritical for someone who drank heavily in college to warn you about excessive drinking? Or for a parent who engaged in casual, unprotected sex at your age to tell you that you ought to abstain until marriage? Or are they just drawing on hard-won experience, including the experience of seeing people they once knew screw up their lives, if they survived at all? After all, who understands the dangers of binge drinking more than a recovering alcoholic, and who has more insight into I-want-to-share-my-love-with-you postprom sex than a thirty-two-year-old single mom with a sixteen-year-old daughter? (Do the math.)

If the flaws of the messenger don't discredit the message, the flip side is that sincerity doesn't substitute for facts, logic, and a connection to reality. The earnest, pure sincerity of the speaker doesn't transform a bad argument into a good one. If it did, we might actually have to listen to Hollywood types when they talk about world economics.

But in our nonjudgmental society, hypocrisy remains one of the last really horrid sins, often treated as worse than lying or corruption. "Hypocrite" remains one of the worst things you can call someone—worse even than "neoconservative zombie." As a result, the charge of hypocrisy is often used as a trump card to win arguments by discrediting one's opponent. Unfortunately, it is also used to blow off a lot of good advice.

Dismissing an argument because of the speaker's hypocrisy is an easy way to score points, but it is what's known as an ad hominem argument—an attack on the individual rather than his ideas. It's tempting, because it allows you to seize the moral high grounds, but it's a lazy tactic. Lazy because it substitutes moral preening for asking whether the argument actually makes sense. It's also lazy because it allows you to effortlessly ignore almost everything grown-ups say since, as a rule, none of them meets the standards of perfection demanded by idealists who apply the hypocrisy label like a scarlet letter of shame.

The problem is that people are not easily divided into saints and sinners. Most of them are more complicated and more interesting, a mixture of strengths, weaknesses, insights, and blind spots. If you demand perfection, you'll be disappointed. If you decide only to listen to perfect people, you'll find that you are pretty much on your own.

On a related note: Judith Martin, better known as Miss

Manners, says that "hypocrisy is not generally a social sin, but a virtue."[114]

One of the worst ideas to come out of the sixties is the belief that good manners are phony because they are inauthentic and insincere. Oddly enough, this is treated as a profound insight, even though it should be obvious that manners are the oil that allows society to survive the frictions of having to be in the same room with people you can't stand.

Good manners include being polite to people who annoy you, smiling and shaking the hands of people you think are jackasses, pretending to be grateful for presents you don't like, and acting interested when your uncle tells his boring stories and lame jokes. They also mean being kind to people we do not know and putting guests and strangers at their ease.

Is this hypocrisy? It is civilization, and you ought to try it.

RULE 30

Zero tolerance = zero common sense.

Zero-tolerance policies are the polar opposite of developing a moral compass, because they don't require any thought at all. They are especially popular among the slow, the lazy, and the bureaucratic. Try using your brain instead.

The roll call of inanities grows every year:

The kindergartner who was suspended for bringing in a dinosaur-shaped plastic squirt gun, in violation of a zero-tolerance weapons ban.[115] A boy suspended from elementary school for using his finger as a pretend gun and saying, "Bang";[116] an eleven-year-old girl suspended for doodling stick-figures of her teachers with arrows through their heads.[117]

At one bastion of zero-tolerance senselessness, an eight-year-old third-grader was suspended for seven days after his mother packed a butter knife in his lunch along with some peanut butter and jelly;[118] at another school an honor student was expelled for carrying a Swiss army knife; and in Texas, a high school baseball player was busted for having an eight-inch-long souvenir baseball bat on the front seat of his car—school officials decided it met the written definition of a weapon. These officials ignored the real aluminum bats that he was carrying in his trunk.[119]

"Nature," as H. L. Mencken so insightfully put it, "abhors a moron."[120] The same obviously cannot be said of school boards who often hire them as principals.

In Indiana, an eighth-grader who realized that he had inadvertently brought a Swiss army knife to school in his jacket pocket turned it in to the office as soon as he arrived at school, but was suspended for ten days anyway. The principal recommended that he be expelled, even though the student had told the truth and done the right thing.[121] Assuming that the point of the no-weapons rule was to keep knives out of school, it had succeeded when the boy turned it in. The message his suspension sent to other students was probably to keep any weapons hidden and as far away from administrators as possible.

In Georgia, a sixth-grader named Ashley Smith was suspended from school for two weeks when administrators decided that her Tweety Bird key chain violated the district's zero-tolerance weapons policy.[122]

A fan of Tweety Bird who runs her own Tweety Bird Web site, Ashley insisted that the tiny chain couldn't hurt anyone. But school administrators told reporters: "A chain like the one in question can have any number of devices attached to it and it becomes a very dangerous weapon." Virtually a weapon of mass destruction.

This sort of dunderheadedness extends to the enforcement of drug policies. Some pencil-necked administrative idiots believe that medications like Midol and Advil should be treated with the same urgency and seriousness as heroin. Rules, after all, are rules, and administrators can't be expected to make distinctions between a hallucinogen and a pain-reliever. So fifteen middle-school students were suspended and required to attend "drug awareness classes and counseling" for passing around and tasting an Alka-Seltzer tablet. In West Virginia a student who brought a cough drop to school was deemed to be in violation of her school's drug policy.[123]

In Louisiana, the Bossier Parish School Board voted to expel high school student Amanda Stiles for a year for possessing a single tablet of Advil. The over-the-counter pain-reliever was found during a search of Amanda's purse after a teacher received a tip that Amanda had been smoking in school. No cigarettes or lighter was found, but the search nailed the Advil. The superintendent said the suspension was "consistent with the board's zero-tolerance policy."[124]

None of this, of course, is really about keeping children safe or even teaching them how to behave. It is about administrators protecting their backsides.

Instead of encouraging children to exercise sound judgment, zero tolerance shows adults at their most arbitrary and stupid, especially when it punishes students for doing the right thing. Consider this classic report from the BBC:

> *A 12-year-old American girl has been branded a drug dealer after going to the aid of a schoolmate who was suffering an asthma attack.*
>
> *Christine Rhodes shared her inhaler with thirteen-year-old Brandy Dyer after spotting her having breathing problems.*
>
> *She has since been suspended from activities at Mount Airy Middle School in Maryland—and labeled a drug trafficker on her school record.*
>
> *Christine insists that she was only trying to help her friend.*
>
> *"The principle of my school told me that what I did was against school rules, giving drugs to another person." she said.*
>
> *"I was really sad and I was crying because I thought she was trying to say that I shouldn't have helped her and let her stay there and almost die."*
>
> *Brandy believes she would not have survived the asthma attack if Christine had not come to her rescue.*
>
> *She said: "If Christine had not given me that inhaler they told me at the hospital that I would have died.*
>
> *"She saved my life and it is unfair that they are giving her these charges."*

> *As a result of Mount Airy's decision, Christine is banned from taking part in school activities for three years. . . ."*[125]

A younger cousin of the zero-tolerance regimes is the push to ban sodas and snack foods from schools as a means of fighting childhood obesity. The assumption behind the soda ban apparently is that if Mountain Dew is unavailable at school, the little Fat Alberts won't be able to find it anywhere else. And, as one worrier earnestly explained to me, we simply can't take the risk of teaching children to exercise good judgment.

That makes perfect sense: how can adults expect kids to use common sense when they are afraid to use it themselves? Don't make those adults your role models.

RULE 31

Naked people look different in real life.

Hollywood's enthusiasm for hyperskinniness has led to something called the "lollipop look," in which a celebrity is so emaciated that her head looks too large for her bony body. But don't make the mistake of thinking that this skeletal look is either normal or glamorous, unless your definition of glamour includes starvation, bingeing and purging, gastric bypass surgery, and debilitating and wasting diseases.

And never make the mistake of confusing the celebrity body image with how real people's bodies actually look.

This may be difficult to realize because yours may be the first generation in the history of mankind to pass through adolescence without seeing anyone naked in person. The key words here are "in person," because of course you can access 100,000 nude pictures with the click of a mouse. But at least you've been sheltered from ever having to see a naked classmate in the shower after gym class. Apparently, that's just too much reality for you to handle.

It was not always so. For generations, group showering was just a part of life, a routine that emphasized basic hygiene, common sense, and the reality of puberty: if you didn't shower, you'd stink. It was also an early reality check: we learned that bodies weren't perfect, that they came in various sizes, stages of growth, and variations. This sort of knowledge actually is useful, especially when it comes to deciding what's normal and what is a freak of nature.

But some years ago the geniuses who run your school decided that no matter how sweaty or rancid you might be, you
wouldn't have to take showers after gym class. Eventually that
idea spread to a lack of showering after any athletic event—
which, in spite of deodorants and body sprays, leads to some
very long and ripe rides home on the team bus.

Of course, this insulation from real-world nakedness means
your generation has to get its notions of the human body from
such reliable and trustworthy sources as Hollywood, magazines,
and the Internet. And grown-ups wonder why so many young
women are obsessed with looking like Keira Knightley.

Unfortunately, millions of your peers look at superthin stars
like Mary-Kay Olsen or Lara Flynn Boyle and think they are normal. The rest of us think, *Get those girls a milkshake, a cheeseburger,*
anything.

Year after year, though, celebrities become increasingly
gaunt—the average supermodel is skinnier than 98 percent of
the rest of us. This trend leads to more pressure on people in the
real world to follow suit. The result is a "size zero" world in
which an estimated ten million females and one million males
wrestle with some form of bulimia or anorexia as they struggle
for the withered look of the rich and beautiful.

Except that it's not beautiful. The sticklike arms of the famous actress, the visible rib cages and bony backs aren't sexy . . .
they are *sick,* making the starlets look more like concentration-
camp survivors than feminine goddesses like Marilyn Monroe or
Brigitte Bardot, who actually looked like what nature intended
women to look like (curves and all).

Hollywood body images, however, have made a remarkable
number of women unhappy with the fact that they look like
women. Perhaps inevitably, the fake body images of popular
culture have led to other forms of fakery. Recently, for example,
Katie Couric, the perky anchorwoman, was stripped of twenty
pounds by a simple act of photoshopping.[126] As it turns out, the
camera not only *can* lie, it lies frequently when it comes to the
rich, famous, and would-be skinny.

Even dress labels can lie. When you begin shopping for adult clothes, you may notice that a dress that was once size eight is now labeled size zero, even though neither the dress nor the women who wear it have shrunk an inch. The size has just been "adjusted" to make everybody feel skinnier.

As if that's not enough, some stores have even introduced a size "double zero." As *The Boston Globe* notes, "If vanity sizing continues on this path . . . it is only a matter of time before clothing sizes are available in negative integers."[127] Which would mean what? That women who buy clothes with negative sizes no longer have any physical reality at all? How glamorous.

So by all means stay healthy, exercise, and eat right. But ignore the supermarket tabloids, and remember that once in a while it's all right to have a cheeseburger.

RULE 32

Television is not real life.

Your life is not a sitcom. Your problems will not all be solved in thirty minutes, minus time for commercials. Adults are not as inept and foolish, and children are not as savvy and all-knowing, as they appear to be on television. In real life people actually have to leave the coffee shop to go to jobs, and, in case you haven't figured it out yet, Reality TV isn't reality.

Of course, you know this, right? But then why do you dress like the people on TV, buy stuff they are pushing, and talk about their shows so much? Naturally, you know it's not *real,* but you can be fooled into taking it as an improved version of reality, a sort of Life 6.0.

In the movies, good defeats evil; cosmic justice is served: the bad guys are either in jail, beaten up, or die spectacular, fiery, and deeply satisfying deaths. Romances work out; the boy usually gets the girl after overcoming obstacles that you knew forty minutes into the show would never keep them apart; snotty people get their comeuppance, occasionally involving truck-loads of cow manure; fathers and sons have moving reconciliations; liars are exposed. If there's a sporting event, it usually ends with victory or an inspiring moral victory that brings a tear to the eye. Things work out, conflicts are resolved, the next episode is a new beginning, and usually there are no hangovers. There are other differences too.

On television, you rarely see people reading books, praying, or muddling through the mundane details of life. Nobody has bad acne or unsightly warts, the heroes seldom have double chins, the love interests are love-handle-free, everybody's teeth look good, and nobody ever has unsightly nose hair unless he is the villain, who will end up dying a spectacular fiery death or having a load of cow manure dumped on him.

In other words, television is exactly what your life would be like if you had a scriptwriter to provide you with a steady stream of one-liners, personal trainers to take off the unsightly bulges, an expense account for liposuction and leg waxing, makeup people to give you perfect skin, editors to get rid of the dull bits, teleprompters so you could get the words right, a DVR so you could go back and replay or even redo the mistakes you made, and a director who would make sure that your problems would be more or less worked out by the end of each episode.

In comparison, you may think your actual life, the daily more-or-less-the-same routine, doesn't measure up in either drama, excitement, or the quality of the costars. If you were under the impression that you were entitled to a more elevated experience, you may find this disappointing or even unfair. (See Rule 1.)

Writer Lance Burri observes:

> *Staying home Friday nights, the minutiae of daily routine, washing the dishes, checking homework. Day in, day out. That may be your life. It isn't mine. My life is supposed to be exciting.*
>
> *This is the real effect of popular culture, I think. In the movies, life isn't boring. . . . It's all so neat and clean. So perfect, and it only takes between two and three hours.*
>
> *At some point, not sure when, I learned life isn't like that. Things don't tie up neatly. When one problem is solved, another takes its place. And sometimes the next one doesn't wait for the first one to finish up.*
>
> *There's no sliding along with a lousy job, and still hanging out with your friends at the coffee house all the time. No*

bouncing from girlfriend to girlfriend with no regrets. No undying romantic relationship that stays fresh and exciting day in, day out.

Life is paying the bills, mopping the floor, nursing the headache and wishing the kids would stop fighting just for five minutes.

At some point, I learned how to take a step back, to get a broader perspective on things. What I saw was this: it's those little annoyances, the problems, the struggles, the anxiety, that make it all worthwhile in the end. It's not exciting, it's routine. But, as my younger self would never understand, I love it.

It's not that I've given up. I haven't just "settled." I have learned there's great satisfaction in walking in my front door at night, and sitting down to dinner. Who would have thought? That I have learned this, I think, is what I'm most thankful for.[128]

In other words, it's not so bad.

RULE 33

Be nice to nerds. You may end up working for them. We all could.

I suspect this rule is one of the reasons so many people thought the original fourteen rules were written by Bill Gates, the planet's most famous billionaire nerd. Face it, he was exactly the kind of guy you'd give wedgies and never sit next to at lunch if the cool kids were around.

So there's a life lesson, because think about the stock options he might have traded for your Twinkie.

Most of us remember something else about nerds. They used to be the guys picked last when sides were chosen up on the playground or in gym class. The order in which kids were chosen was a reliable barometer of popularity and status. To be chosen first was a sign that you were the most athletic or most popular guy in the class; to be picked in the lower half was a symbol of social failure; to be chosen last proof of irremediable geekhood. But as bad as this was, choosing up sides is also a valuable life lesson: it is a powerful incentive to be good at *something*. If not at football or volleyball, then at current events, or at foreign languages, drama, or mastering arcane technology. To excel at something was not just a form of sweet revenge; it was also a kind of modest salvation for kids who might not otherwise have fit in. There's a reason Napoleon Dynamite became a cultural icon.

Genuinely successful and popular kids seem to understand

this. Often, the kids who pick on nerds are the more marginal and insecure wannabes who are trying to prop up their status by emphasizing their superiority to the social untouchables. These are the kids who are afraid to match themselves against the biggest, brightest, coolest kids in school, but try to prove their coolness by picking on the weakest and most vulnerable. Being nasty to the nerds may get you a laugh, but choosing to harass them really says far more about you than it does about the kid you just stuffed in the locker.

Even so, never underestimate how hard it is to be considered a geek or how genuinely cruel some kids can be to others. Writer Paul Graham notes that no one works harder than American kids at being popular.

> *Navy SEALs and neurosurgery residents seem slackers by comparison. They occasionally take vacations; some even have hobbies. An American teenager may work at being popular every waking hour, 365 days a year. . . .*
>
> *[E]very effort they make to do things "right" is also, consciously or not, an effort to be more popular. Nerds don't realize this.*[129]

Maybe because they have other things to think about. Maybe because they think there is nothing they can do about it. But never underestimate how toughening it must be to endure the slings and arrows of adolescent unpopularity. The real world holds few terrors for the nerd who has survived seventh grade.

Remember this too: what passes for cool in school doesn't always translate into cool later in life. Adult life tends to have a different hierarchy than tenth grade (thank God). Some of the traits most highly valued in school will prove to be irrelevant, worthless, and worse. At the same time, some of the skills and talents overlooked among your peers are the ones that will be the most valuable. Graham writes that he found that one of the most common regrets among adults was caring so much about what other people thought. He adds:

> *I think what they really mean . . . is caring what random*
> *people thought of them. Adults care just as much what other peo-*
> *ple think, but they get to be more selective about the other*
> *people. I have about thirty friends whose opinions I care about,*
> *and the opinion of the rest of the world barely affects me. The*
> *problem in high school is that your peers are chosen for you by*
> *accidents of age and geography, rather than by you based on re-*
> *spect for their judgment."*[130]

This is part of recognizing that most of the things that you
are worrying about now are crap: what you wear, what you buy,
what the girl sitting behind you thinks of your butt, or whether
you have the slimmest camera phone. Twenty years from now
you might remember the girl you wanted to go out with who sat
behind you in history, but you won't care that much about her.

There are, however, even better reasons to be nice to nerds: it
is the decent thing to do and helps develop the habit of treating
others well, especially people who may for the moment not be
your social equals. A recent survey of CEOs of major companies, for example, found that the executives unanimously agreed
that the way people treat waiters, secretaries, and security guards
was a reliable guide to their character. Bill Swanson, the CEO of
Raytheon, says one of the most reliable unwritten rules of business is: "A person who is nice to you but rude to the waiter, or to
others, is not a nice person."[131]

And, given the number of people who have been passed over
for jobs because they are jerks to the receptionist, such a person is
also not very smart.

RULE 34

Winners have a philosophy of life. So do losers.

Denis Waitley notes: "The winners in life think constantly in terms of I can, I will, and I am. Losers, on the other hand, concentrate their waking thoughts on what they should have or would have done, or what they can't do."[132]

The difference in the philosophies is not hard to spot, as in the following pairs of quotes:

Green Bay Packer legend Vince Lombardi: "Life's battles don't always go to the stronger or faster man. But sooner or later the man who wins is the man who thinks he can."[133]

Anticompetition education guru Alfie Kohn: "Competition teaches children to envy winners, dismiss losers and mistrust everyone."[134]

"A man can be as great as he wants to be," said Lombardi. "If you believe in yourself and have the courage, the determination, the dedication, the competitive drive and if you are willing to sacrifice the little things in life and pay the price for the things that are worthwhile, it can be done."[135]

"I learned my first game at a birthday party," says Kohn. "The game was musical chairs. You remember it, X players scramble for X-minus one chairs until the music stops. In every round a child is eliminated until at the end, only one child is left triumphantly seated while everyone else is left standing on the sidelines, excluded from play, unhappy . . . losers."[136]

Lombardi won three NFL titles.
Kohn was traumatized by . . . *musical chairs.*

Losers usually hate competition because they hate to lose. They avoid being tested because they are more concerned about feeling bad than about building a skill or achieving a goal. Losers make excuses, blame others, confuse their intentions with performance—they are always meaning to do something, but never actually do it. They easily become discouraged, often magnifying the problems and obstacles they face, so they develop the habit of quitting.

Of course, nobody wants to be a loser, so they rationalize— and along the way embrace the philosophy of losing, a doctrine that comes complete with its own gurus, dogmas, traditions, and even political parties. Losers embrace the convenient and self-validating idea that their lack of success is somebody else's fault—society's or The Man's or the System's, or else they blame other popular targets of Slacker Nation. After all, what else could explain the world's failure to recognize the center-of-the universe specialness represented by all those gold stars and trophies?

Often losers develop a finely honed sense of their place and fight hard against letting others try to climb out of it. They find a way to smugly dismiss the values that contribute to winning: Every burnout can tell you how uncool it is for other kids to study hard, practice hard, or work hard. In the central city, academic achievement is sometimes derided as "acting white"; success becomes an act of racial betrayal. (Does that mean that dysfunction and failure are expressions of racial solidarity?) Rednecks are just as adamant in turning on anyone who dares to think he is better than guys in dirty T-shirts hanging around the trailer park. You can always spot the losers: Instead of admiring the success of others, they're likely to think it's the result of favoritism, luck, or some other sort of unfair advantage. They are as unwilling to admit that somebody else deserves a promotion as they are to admit that they don't.

Losers also convince themselves that they don't really want to be winners. "I don't really want to be a great artist," a coworker once told me. "I just want to be an average artist." (You can substitute engineer, accountant, actor, lawyer, or baseball player.)

In other words, they settle. They settle for "good enough"— the types who watch the clock until the second hand reaches five, who gravitate to jobs where they don't have to accomplish anything, overcome challenges, or meet difficult goals, but instead put in their eight hours, keep the machine running, and wait to collect their pensions. (This, by the way, exactly describes most public-education bureaucrats.)

A particular sort of loser confuses short-term pleasure with long-term satisfaction. He has high self-esteem but low self-control. Consider Olympic loser Bode Miller.

"I just want to go out and rock, and, man, I rocked here," Miller told the Associated Press after the 2006 Torino Olympics. "I'm comfortable with what I accomplished. I came in here to race as hard as I could. I got to party and socialize at the Olympic level."[137]

His record on the slopes?

> *Combined: Disqualified*
> *Super-G: Did Not Finish*
> *Giant Slalom: Sixth*
> *Slalom: Did Not Finish*
> *Downhill: Fifth*

"At least I don't have to go down to Torino for the medal ceremony," he said after being disqualified in the combined.[138]

But Bode thought he rocked. And he got to party, at great

length and, if the reports are to be believed, far into the night when other competitors were resting up for the competition. Undeniably, he is a gifted athlete who may have a lot of success later in life. But, dude, the guy left the Olympics as a loser—not because he lacked the skills or ability, but because he had the attitude of a loser. Instead of recognizing the opportunity and seizing the moment, Bode hit the bars. That shot glass should look good over the mantelpiece twenty years from now.

In contrast, winners are not afraid to be tested and don't shy away from competition. What they bring that losers don't is focus, preparation, and perseverance. Even among people who actually have some sort of ambition, not everyone is prepared to pay the price in terms of effort, sacrifice, and sweat. Winners are; they know how to shut off the white noise of distraction and negativity and to ignore the roommate who tells them to skip practice because a friend of a friend knows some hot twins who'll be partying at the bars tonight.

Losers buy lottery tickets because they think success is a matter of luck. Winners know that it never hurts to be lucky, but they also know that their success is up to them, and they are willing to take responsibility for it.

My experience is that winners usually are trusted by the people with whom they work, and often liked as well because they can be relied upon in a crisis. Winners attract the support and loyalty of people who want to be close to success and the values it represents. Losers tend to attract fellow whiners.

While winners will often take responsibility for cleaning up other people's messes, you can usually spot the losers in any class, team, or organization: they are the complainers, the experts in spotting the flaws in other people's plans, and they can always be counted on to point out all of the things that could ever possibly go wrong. They draw their inspiration from the editorial writers who come down from the hills after the battle to shoot the wounded.

Winners, on the other hand, draw their inspiration from Teddy Roosevelt.

> *It is not the critic who counts, nor the man who points out how the strong man stumbled or where the doer of deeds could have done them better. The credit belongs to the man who is actually in the arena; whose face is marred by dust and sweat and blood; who strives valiantly . . . who knows the great enthusiasms, the great devotions, and spends himself in a worthy cause; who, at best, knows the triumph of high achievement; and who, at the worst, if he fails, at least fails while daring greatly, so that his place shall never be with those cold and timid souls who know neither victory nor defeat.*[139]

. . . and who probably end up with jobs as guidance counselors in your high school.

RULE 35

If your butt has its own zip code, it's not because Mc-Donald's forced you to eat all those Big Macs. If you smoke, it's not Joe Camel's fault.

The key to avoiding the loser philosophy of life is to resist the temptation to blame other people for your problems or your choices. Not blaming other people for what you put into your own mouth is a good place to start. As for smoking: I'm already on record as saying that smoking makes you look moronic. The only thing more moronic than actually smoking is blaming a cartoon for making you start. Have a little pride.

More than a decade ago, when a man filed an equal-protection complaint against McDonald's for not having seats big enough for his backside, Mike Royko wrote that this complainer "was not born with a 60-inch waist and an enormous butt. After a certain point, he created himself and his butt. They are his responsibility."[140] But Royko was writing in a kinder, gentler, less legally creative time.

Someday, Caesar Barber may be remembered as a pioneer in the campaign to convince Americans that they are never responsible for anything. The 270-pound Barber made legal history when he sued McDonald's and every other fast-food joint where he was a regular consumer, including Burger King, KFC, and Wendy's, blaming them for making him obese.[141]

Only a few years ago, this was all the stuff of parody. In 2000

The Onion, a newspaper devoted to satirical spoofs, ran a gag story headlined, HERSHEY'S ORDERED TO PAY OBESE AMERICANS $135 BILLION. According to the story, the candy merchant was found to have "knowingly and willfully" marketed to children "rich, fatty candy bars containing chocolate and other ingredients of negligible nutritional value" while "spiking" them with "peanuts, crisped rice and caramel to increase consumer appeal."[142] Three years earlier, Mark F. Bernstein wrote a parody in *The Wall Street Journal,* entitled "A Big Fat Target." It singled out "Wisconsin Cheese Lords" and junk-food marketers accusing them of clogging our arteries."[143]

Bernstein admitted that as long as Americans believed that people exercise free will in choosing what they eat, his tongue-in-cheek attack on Big Cheese had to seem "a bit preposterous." But he concluded: "It is too hot to exercise. Dieting demands willpower, and why bother if you're just a victim? Come on, America. Get off that couch and sue."

But you cannot, as they say, make this stuff up anymore.

The fifty-seven-year-old Barber, who continued to frequent fast-food outlets three or four times a week even after suffering two heart attacks, claimed that he had been bamboozled by the (completely truthful) claim that McDonald's burger was 100 percent beef, which he took to mean that "it was good for you. I thought the food was OK. The fast food industry has wrecked my life. I was conned, I was fooled. I was tricked." For this moon-faced stupidity, Caesar hoped to be paid at least a million dollars.

His suit was succeeded by the lawsuit filed by two teenage couch-soufflés whose nearly daily trips to McDonald's had contributed to their gargantuan waistlines. The judge tossed the case, declaring, "Nobody is forced to eat at McDonald's."[144] He also pointed out that "It's not the place of the law to protect them from their own excesses." But the dismissal was only a temporary reprieve for Big Fat, because there are simply too many folks waiting to feed at the trough of nutritional correctness.

There are literally thousands of counselors, bureaucrats, nutrition activists, and trial lawyers whose livelihood depends on your thinking of yourself as a victim of the fast-food conspiracy—the sort of people who argue that "toy promotions" and "happy meals" are a lethal combination. (Ralph Nader calls a McDonald's burger a "weapon of mass destruction."[145]) To protect you from yourself, Yale professor and antifat activist Kelly Brownell is pushing for "Twinkie taxes," laws regulating restaurants, age limits for certain products, tobacco-style restrictions on some foods, including price controls, and even outright bans on some popular foods in schools.[146]

If the trial lawyers are ever to get their hands into the quite-deep pockets of the fast-food business, they will have to move people away from what überlawyer John Banzhaf refers to as "these arguments about personal responsibility . . . all these platitudes about, 'people should eat less,' 'responsibility,' all this crap!"[147] In other words, you can't be trusted to decide what you eat.

Skip Spitzer of the Pesticide Action Network chimes in, calling the very idea of personal responsibility "a cultural construct."[148] As if anything could be more of a cultural construct than lawsuits against the makers of nachos and Ding Dongs for making kids fat.

Unfortunately, though, when the stakes are high enough, people are willing to believe almost anything, especially if those people work for the government.

The federal government, for example, has created a $125-million program "to persuade children 9 through 13 to become physically active."[149] This is a $125-million get-out-and-play program in which the federal government tells kids to put the Nintendo down, get off the couch, and go outside and play. Isn't that what your mom used to do for free?

"It's a beautiful day," she'd say, "turn off that bleeping television and go ride your bike or something. And no more Oreos until after you've eaten dinner." And she'd make you eat your vegetables. Now it's a federal program.

The assumption here is that unless the federal government tells you to do these things, you simply won't be able to figure it out on your own. Apparently we're also supposed to assume that youngsters who tune out millions of parents, blow off thousands of gym teachers, and ignore the incentives of being attractive to the opposite sex will somehow listen to the federal government. What's next? A $125-million program on the benefits of wearing warm socks?

Well, why not? If you can't figure out what to put into your mouth or that it's a good idea to walk around the block once in a while, how can you possibly be entrusted to make any other decision without the advice of Big Nanny?

By now the pattern of nannyism is familiar: crisis + villain = rules + litigation. In this case the crisis is obesity; the villain is fast food; the regulations include snack taxes and soda bans; and the litigation is against restaurants, marketers, and who knows who else for enticing helpless children to the fleshpots of the Big 'n Tasty with fries.

An alternative to all of this, of course, would be for people to simply exercise enough personal responsibility and self-control to say no. You could start with yourself. This would spoil all of the fun for hand-wringing editorialists, posturing politicians, food bureaucrats, and predatory trial lawyers.

But at least you'd be able to decide for yourself whether you want that enchilada with cheese.

RULE 36

You are not immortal.

Contrary to what you might expect, there is very little risk that you will die of boredom. You could, however, very easily die of stupidity. Right now you are going through the most dangerous period of your life, at least until menopause or midlife crisis, when you might be tempted to move to Arizona and take up hang gliding. All the forty-year-olds I know find it amazing that they managed to survive the dumb things they did as teenagers, from streaking to tequila shots, when they were under the impression that they were invulnerable.

The biggest threats you face are euphemistically called "risky behaviors," most of which involve drugs, drinking, sex, and cars. You've heard the cliché "None of us is as smart as all of us," but when it comes to driving, nobody is as dumb, reckless, and irresponsible as all of you; the IQs and common sense of teenagers decline in direct proportion to the number of them riding in car. This is the precise moment when it is important that you have chosen the right friends, or at least the right people to hang around with.

If you are under the impression that living fast, dying young, and leaving a beautiful corpse are romantic, you obviously haven't seen one of your peers at room temperature lately.

They don't look glamorous, or even tragic; they are usually blue-gray and cold and are often quite messy. Whoever came up with the phrase "going out in a blaze of glory" never visited a burn unit, or saw what was zipped into a body bag after a fiery car crash. There is little romance in being identified by your dental records.

Don't assume that everybody gets it.

In a rural town in Wisconsin last year, a group of teenagers—two of them sixteen years old—sat around a park drinking beer, then jumped into a car, sped out onto the highway, and ended up killing five people, including themselves and an elderly couple heading home from a doctor's appointment.[150] The death of five people in a car accident was appalling enough, but the aftermath was what shocked the community.

The friends of the dead teenagers memorialized the tragedy by going to the crash scene and . . . drinking, even leaving cans of Pabst Blue Ribbon beer as a makeshift memorial. "See ya later Mike!" read one can, signed, "Tom." Written on another empty beer can: "This ones for you." [sic]

Nearby, somebody had written on a cardboard sign: "Live hard. Party Hard. Party to the death."

"And never mind, I guess, who you take with you," commented *Milwaukee Journal Sentinel* columnist Mike Nichols.[151]

The sixteen-year-old driver who lost control of the car had a blood-alcohol level twice the legal limit, even for someone legally able to drink. The accident left behind five separate grieving families—fathers, mothers, brothers, sisters, children, grandchildren, uncles, aunts, cousins.

There were five funerals. There were no parties.

This is one of the reasons your parents may seem so hung up and stressed out; they know that their biggest job is just to get you through all this, and you don't always make it easy. Ironically, one of the consequences of the bubble-wrapping of children over the last few decades has been a revolt against the safe-but-dull regime; a generation that has been protected from dodgeball seems increasingly attracted to X-treme sports and edge-of-the-envelope risk taking. Maybe a life spent in bubble wrap has reinforced the impression that you are exempt from bruises. You aren't.

When you get behind the wheel of a car, assume that every other driver is an idiot, moments away from committing an act of vehicular madness. You are sharing the road with drivers who apply makeup, pick their teeth or their nose, fiddle with their cell phones and/or laptops, eye up scantily clad joggers, and reach for moving objects like their girlfriends, which happened to be the cause of my most spectacular accident when I was seventeen. You need to behave accordingly.

If you are a teenager, expect that you will be held absolutely responsible for any accident. You need to avoid the temptation to blame any other factor, person, condition, or driver for any scrapes, collisions, or crashes. If you are not willing to do that, your parents have the right (and obligation) to pull your driving privileges, take away the car, and cancel the insurance. They don't want to visit you in the morgue.

RULE 37

Being connected does not mean you aren't clueless.

Even with your IM, cell phones, iPods, satellite television,
DVRs, and CD players, you can still be oblivious about what is
happening around you. Do you have any clue what your parents' lives are like? What they did today? What your brothers or
sisters did? Even worse, when you shut off all that noise, the
void amid the sudden silence could be the real you.

Modern media allow you to fill your head 24/7 with an artificial
life. But at least recognize that's what it is: artificial, as in fake,
make-believe. While surfing the vast matrix of modern technology, you can easily wind up living in a world of synthetic emotions
and manufactured drama. As a master of multitasking, you have
figured out how to use much of the media—music, instant-
messaging, even Google searches—while doing things like homework. But stimulation is not individuality, and noise is not
personality, and sometimes it is real people who get reduced to
background white noise amid the digital clutter.

How quaint that two or three decades ago experts worried
about the effects of television on the brain development of
young children. A 2005 survey by the Kaiser Family Foundation
found that kids inhabited a world of digital saturation, spending
an average of 6.5 hours *a day* with various media.[152] But even
this understates their exposure, because more than a quarter of
the time, children were using more than one medium. So the

foundation estimated that they were actually exposed to the daily equivalent of 8.5 hours of media content, crammed into the 6.5 hours they were "connected."

Those 8.5 hours should be compared to the hour a day our "overburdened" and "overworked" kids spent on homework and the mere half hour a day they spent doing chores[153] (and since this was self-reported, those numbers deserve to be regarded with some skepticism).

Despite what some antitechnology troglodytes might think, this isn't all bad: at least you are no longer couch potatoes who passively absorb the wit and wisdom of *Saved by the Bell*—you now interact with your electronic universe. But the downside is that you probably spend less and less time sitting next to or talking with real people.[154] That sort of eye-to-eye, in-the-same-room interaction has been the basis of families, friendships, and society since guys named Gog first learned to communicate interesting news about woolly mammoths.

The Kaiser study found that kids who spent a lot of time connected to media said they hung out a lot with their parents, but the quality of those interactions is questionable. Were they having dinner together and talking about the details of daily life? Or merely occupying the same physical space but different psychic universes? Nearly two-thirds of young people (63 percent) reported that the television was on during dinner. In a majority of homes, the TV was on "most of the time." So what really gets the attention? How can Dad compete with *The O.C.*?

The temptation of media saturation, of course, is to treat people in the actual world—family members, professors, coworkers—as if they are TV; you may listen to them with half a mind while you are also answering e-mails, trolling search engines, or playing video games. The addiction to multitasking has gotten so bad that some colleges now ban laptops from classrooms, because professors found they were being treated like background noise rather than real people in real time.[155]

All of this connectedness can also erode self-reliance. "You get used to things happening right away," says psychologist

Bernardo J. Carducci, a professor at Indiana University Southeast. The world of instant communication, instant results, and instant gratification has consequences. "You not only want the pizza now, you generalize that expectation to other domains, like friendship and intimate relationships. You become frustrated and impatient easily. You become unwilling to work out problems. And so relationships fail—perhaps the single most powerful experience leading to depression."[156]

And then there's the content of the media swarm: the billions of bits of information, the unregulated flow of data, information, science, math, violence, pornography, truth, fraud, and pettifoggery streaming through headphones, high-speed connections, and video screens.

If there ever really was a battle over parental control, it is over and spectacularly lost. Marking the Great Surrender, most eight-to-eighteen-year-olds said their parents had no rules about watching TV. Despite ongoing controversies about violent video games, the Kaiser study found that only 5 percent of older teenagers said their parents had any rules at all about what they play; only 25 percent of younger teens had any rules. On the issue of games like Grand Theft Auto, somewhere between 75 and 95 percent of America's parents had wilted like overcooked pasta. (And yes, the kids do play the games. In the Kaiser study, 62 percent of seventh-to-twelfth-graders said they had played Grand Theft Auto.)

In the same study, only a quarter of young people said there were any parental controls or filters on their computers; only 14 percent of parents checked parental advisories on music their children bought (or had the slightest idea that their little boys were listening to lyrics about bitches, hos, and worse); and only one in ten even bothered to check the ratings on games.[157]

In other words, in the digital age, you are on your own.

RULE 38

Look people in the eye when you meet them . . .

. . . especially if you want to show them that you are not the sort of sulky, self-centered, spoiled brat they've been reading about in this book.

Lord Chesterfield was a savvy, hardheaded English aristocrat who lived from 1694 to 1773 and wrote a famous series of letters to his son and godson, advising them on manners, morals, and making their way in the world. So this quotation is more than two hundred years old, but it describes a habit that still annoys the bejabbers out of people like me:

> _I have seen many people, who while you are speaking to them, instead of looking at, and attending to you, fix their eyes upon the ceiling, or some other part of the room, look out of the window, play with a dog, twirl their snuff-box, or pick their nose. Nothing discovers a little, futile, frivolous mind more than this, and nothing is so offensively ill-bred._[158]

There's actually an even worse habit. The fastest way to offend someone is to look over his shoulder when he is being introduced to you. You'll meet people like this soon enough: even when they are shaking your hand, they will look around the room, checking to see whether there is somebody more important or interesting than you are. The message they are sending couldn't be clearer: "I can't be bothered to pay attention to you."

Unfortunately, this sort of attitude seems to have become another generational marker. Jean Twenge cites studies suggesting that young people are far less interested than previous generations in making a good impression or observing basic rules of civility when they interact with adults. MIT psychologist and sociologist Sherry Turkle told *USA Today:* "They're tuned out in some ways to the social graces around them and the people in their lives, in their physical realm, and tuned in to the people they're with virtually."[159]

(Quick Useful Tip: don't try to listen to music with your iPod earbud or send text messages while an adult is trying to talk to you, unless you want to get an unexpected lesson in what the inside of your iPod or cell phone looks like.)

But ignoring or brushing off people around you is the sort of thing that Chesterfield had in mind when he also warned his son that "an injury is much sooner forgotten than an insult."[160]

A corollary rule: it is highly unlikely that you are the smartest person in the room, so don't act like it. Again, there's nothing new about this. Chesterfield warned his son:

> *Never yield to that temptation, which, to most young men, is very strong, of exposing other people's weaknesses and infirmities, for the sake either of diverting the company, or of showing your own superiority. You may get the laugh on your side by it for the present; but you will make enemies by it forever; and even those who laugh with you then, will, upon reflection, fear, and consequently hate you.*[161]

It is also worth remembering that while the most fascinating thing in the world is talking about yourself, it is also what is most boring to other people.

So learn to listen, to pay attention to others, and to treat them with respect. This will pay off in several respects: People are actually much more interesting than you think. Those that have lived longer and had more experiences than you might even be more interesting than you are.

RULE 39

People in black-and-white movies were in color in real life. And no, the world did not begin when you were born.

At the University of Washington recently, the student senate voted down a proposal to honor Gregory "Pappy" Boyington, a 1933 graduate of the university who was awarded the Congressional Medal of Honor for his service commanding the famed Black Sheep squadron during World War II. One student objected that the decorated Marine was not "an example of the sort of person UW wants to produce." Another student sniped, "We don't need to honor any more rich white males."

But, as *The Wall Street Journal* later pointed out, Boyington was "neither white nor especially rich." He was, in fact, an American Indian who raised his three children as a single parent.[162]

What you had on display here was several young people who had passed through an expensive public education system, if not utterly unaware of American history, at least without any sense of the sacrifices others had made so that pampered college students would be free to say foolish things at student-senate meetings.

Don't smirk.

In 2001, according to the National Assessment of Education Progress, nearly six in ten high school seniors scored below "basic" in American history, meaning they were pretty much clueless about anything that happened before 1986.[163] Nearly a third of seniors lacked even a basic grasp of civics.

"More young Americans could name the Three Stooges than the three branches of government," quipped David Eisenhower, the grandson of the president (Dwight Eisenhower, in case you were wondering).[164]

He wasn't joking. A recent survey found that 22 percent of Americans could name all five members of the Simpson cartoon family while only one person in the one thousand surveyed could name all five freedoms guaranteed in the First Amendment.[165] (The five Simpsons are Bart, Lisa, Homer, Marge, and Maggie. The five freedoms are freedom of speech, religion, press, and assembly and the right to petition for redress of grievances.)

The ignorance runs deep. When high school seniors were asked to pick a U.S. ally in World War II from a list of countries, more than half chose Italy, Germany, or Japan, which just happen to be the countries we were fighting against. There's a relatively simple explanation for why students don't know this: nobody bothered to teach them.

The typical product of public education has only the vaguest notion of the country's past, except perhaps a fuzzy idea that our freedoms were won by a collection of worthies that included English teachers with ACLU cards, the International Garment Workers Union, the suffragettes, and Florence Kelley, the founder of the National Consumer's League. They are also given a smattering of interesting knowledge about the production of maize and legislation passed in the nineteenth century by guys who looked like they wore dead squirrels on their faces.

But the real problem is that, being layered with political correctness, most history textbooks are dull, flat, and eye-glazingly boring even by the standards of modern educationist dreck.

In *The Language Police: How Pressure Groups Restrict What Students Learn,* Diane Ravitch describes the bloodless, inoffensive pap that fills the modern textbook:

> *Stories that have no geographical location. . . . Stories in which all conflicts are insignificant. Stories in which men are fearful and women are brave. Stories in which older people are*

never ill. Stories in which children are obedient, never disrespectful, never get into dangerous situations, never confront problems that cannot be easily solved. Stories in which blind people and people with physical disabilities need no assistance from anyone because their handicaps are not handicaps. . . . Stories about the past in which historical accuracy is ignored. . . . Stories in which everyone is happy almost all the time.[166]

In other words, stories with all the blood, drama, personality, and interest drained out of them. Educrats try rationalizing all of this by arguing that it's not important to learn mere facts about history; that it is more important to learn to "think historically." But how do you think about history without knowing what happened?

Fortunately, there is an antidote to this diet of intellectual tofu. I was lucky enough to be in Gettysburg for the 140th anniversary of the battle and to walk the ground where Robert E. Lee, supremely confident, watched his desperate gamble fail; where a handful of exhausted men made a desperate charge to save Little Round Top and the Union flank, and General Pickett led his tragic last charge.

And I wondered: *How in God's name did they ever make this boring? How did our schools decide this wasn't worth teaching and that if it was worth teaching, it should be taught badly, carefully gutted of anything that might capture the imagination of children?*

So while educationists were wringing their hands about their failure to interest students in history, my wife, my son Alex, and I were standing at the "Angle" on Cemetery Ridge, where the Confederacy reached its high-water mark and was broken. "This is so cool," Alex said. "I want to know everything about the battle." You'd never convince him that history is boring. Unfortunately schools have been doing a damn good job of convincing students of exactly that.

RULE 40

Despite the billion-dollar campaign to turn your brain into tapioca pudding, try to learn to think clearly and logically.

Ideas have consequences, so learn to take them seriously. This won't be easy in an age dominated by feather-headed emotionalism; these days learning to employ linear thought is a subversive act. Learn to distinguish facts from wishful thinking, reason from rationalization, and when you encounter bureaucratic blah, blah, blah, learn to ask, "So what?" (This always throws them off their game.)

G. K. Chesterton once wrote that the problem when people stop believing in God is not that they believe in nothing, but that they will *believe anything at all.* The same can be said about people who've forgotten how to think.

They'll believe in the healing powers of St. Didimus's foreskin, or that an alien spaceship is parked behind the Hale-Bopp comet (a tenet of the Heaven's Gate cult); they'll buy into conspiracy theories about September 11, think O. J. Simpson was innocent, or even believe that Madonna can act.

People who've lost the knack of linear thought are basically defenseless, blown whichever way the wind or the fads of the day happen to be blowing, chasing one empty banner after another. So they are easy prey and dupes for charlatans with credentials, romantic wishful thinking, and rhetoric dressed up as science—one of the reasons why the media and public are so apt to buy into the latest scary study, only to find out six months later that the earlier scare was bogus or overhyped (but where would the media be without a crisis—"shark attacks at your child's day care . . . film at eleven!").

An even-greater challenge is posed by our rampant non-judgmentalism, the notion that nothing is inherently good or bad because all values are relative; so, of course, all views are valid, and who are we to say? In this world, the worst sin—the cardinal, unforgivable sin—is to be "judgmental."

But this is a cop-out, with the added disadvantage of being false. For example, the statement that "no opinion is any more valid than any other" is itself an opinion. And the statement that there are no absolutes is—embarrassingly enough—an absolute itself. It is also lazy, because it spares people the trouble of having to think through their beliefs and arguments. If no idea is better than any other, why bother? Why argue? Why think at all?

But there's another problem with this posture of nonjudg-mental relativism: nobody actually believes it.

You'll run into people who will say things like: "What is true for me might not be true for you," or "because I think it is right, that doesn't mean it is also right for others." But when you push them, you will always find that they believe in something . . . if only in the superiority of nonjudgmentalism.

Try this: ask them if their relativism applies to genocide in Rwanda. Is mass murder wrong for them, but a legitimate choice for others? What about the denial of the basic rights of women in some cultures? The Nazi death camps? Stalin's use of starvation to pacify the Ukraine? The Spanish Inquisition? The lynchings of blacks in the South?

If not, why not? Personal preference? But if there is no moral standard except your personal preference, why should you think your personal preference is any better than anyone else's? Who are we to say?

Is freedom of religion preferable to putting to death people who pray differently? Is gender equality a better idea than treating women like slaves? Is racial equality morally superior to the racist policies of the South African apartheid regime? If so, why?

Don't confuse relativism with either skepticism or open-mindedness, because those attitudes involve searching for a true answer. Asking questions implies that there is a correct answer and that some things are better and some things worse, although we don't know what they are. Relativism, on the other hand, argues that there is nothing that is absolutely good or bad, that all values are relative.

But if that's true and if you can't appeal to any higher moral principle, if everyone's opinion is as valid as anyone else's, if there is no objective basis for saying that Martin Luther King Jr. was morally superior to Adolf Hitler, then the only way to resolve differences is by force—either by one group imposing its views on the minority or by the minority imposing theirs on the majority.

Multiculturalists will point out that different cultures have different value systems. They will go on to claim that it is something-ocentric to imply that any of these systems is any better than any other. But while cultures may disagree about what is good, the disagreement is never about whether there *is* a good. They disagree about degree, not substance. "Try to imagine a society," writes theologian Peter Kreeft, "where honesty and justice and courage and self-control and faith and hope and charity are *evil,* and lying and cheating and stealing and cowardice and betrayal and addiction and despair and hate are all *good.* You just can't do it."[167]

No society has ever believed that all values are simply a matter of opinion and personal preference . . . until our own.

You don't have to buy into that.

You can start by learning how to talk about ideas.

Despite generations of young people who have relied upon such tactics, rolling your eyes, smirking, and muttering "whatever" are not witty comebacks, much less coherent arguments. This doesn't mean you shouldn't respond to people with different opinions, politics, and religions than you. If you don't agree with something someone has said, by all means, take a stand. Make your case.

But *your feelings are not an argument.*

Calling your opponent a Nazi is not an argument.

Calling him a (fill in the blank)-ist is not a coherent argument.

Make your case with facts, logic, reason, and linear thought. You will rock his world.

RULE 41

You are not the first and you are not the only one who has gone through what you are going through.

You don't want to hear this from your parents, because nobody wants to think he is a walking cliché. Everybody thinks that his problems are unique in the history of emotional trauma, and sufferers are reluctant to admit that others have been there and done that, including what you do when the lights are out, the door is closed, and you think no one is looking.

You are not the first kid to be left out or made fun of, or the first to feel lonely. You are not the first or only kid to be rejected by a member of the opposite sex and feel your insides are being shredded. You aren't the first or only kid to think his face looks like it was hit with a bag of nails and never want to leave his room again. You are not the first or only teenager who has stared at his bedroom ceiling when no one was around, wondering what would become of him.

You are not the first or only teenager who thinks he has deep, dark, and shameful secrets that would shock, horrify, and scandalize his parents and peers. (Probably about 95 percent of your peers have the same secrets.) You aren't the first or only kid who thinks he is a loser or thinks about killing himself or other people. You aren't the first or only kid to cry about silly things, or to feel himself losing control, or to tell his parents he hates them when he really doesn't mean it.

You are a teenager, with all the yuckiness, weirdness, and coolness that implies; and until society decides to lock all of you in a secure room until you turn twenty-two, we all have to deal with it. You'll survive.

RULE 42

Change the oil.

OK, it's not a cosmic issue, but there are quite a few details of life that you will have to master that nobody might get around to mentioning. Changing the oil on your car is one of them. It took me years and several thousands of dollars of costly maintenance and repair bills before it sunk in that I really did have to change the oil regularly, or bad and smoky things would happen to very expensive stuff. Seriously, it never came up in World History, although my son's high school recently sent a flier telling upperclassmen: "If you don't work to control events, they'll control you. Neglect, like bad mistakes, can have disastrous consequences. One of the signs of maturity is the awareness of how neglect can lead to misfortune. You may have to live with the consequences of failing to take timely action." Obviously, that applies to changing the oil, rotating the tires, flossing, and a lot of nonmaintenance life decisions you will face; it's good advice.

Other details that might not get covered:

Tip. If you get good service, add 15 percent to the bill (that's roughly one-sixth). Most of the people waiting on you are paid less than minimum wage, so they rely on tips to survive. One of the secrets of life is that you will get much better service if you tip generously.

Learn to do laundry. Unless you plan to live with your mom forever or are OK with smelling like old socks and moldy underwear. Separate colors. Use cold water.

Learn to cook. Unless you want to spend the rest of your life eating out of a can or eating fast food. You will be amazed at how impressed your significant other will be if you can make something more complicated than cereal.

Save. If you actually start setting aside money in your twenties (and it doesn't have to be that much), you can end up a millionaire. If you take this advice, you have no idea how grateful you will be when you are forty-five years old.

Floss. You don't want to have root-canal surgery. Trust me. Dental pain is on par with passing a gallstone or childbirth. So when you are writhing in agony from a wicked toothache later in life, you will wish your mom had been holding a whip when she told you to brush eight times a day (or was it only three?) and to use floss.

Nose hair. Cut it.

You're welcome.

RULE 43

Don't let the successes of others depress you.

There is a word, borrowed from German, for the pleasure we take in the disappointments and suffering of others: it is *schadenfreude*. Schadenfreude is the basic principle behind 90 percent of Reality TV.

The opposite is a specific kind of jealousy: being depressed by the *good fortune* of others. Envy is an ugly emotion and an even worse lifestyle, and it doesn't get any less ugly when you try to accessorize it as idealism (pretending that your jealousy is a sense of justice or fairness, for example). Unfortunately, it is the common lot of mankind not only to covet your neighbor's ass (I'm using the term here in the biblical sense), but also to be annoyed and irritable if he has an especially nice one.

I learned this one afternoon in a hotel room in Washington, D.C. An acquaintance had recently published a quite successful book and was getting both good reviews and healthy sales. As it happened, the author deserved all of this success, because the book was well-done, timely, and an important addition to the public debate. And so I was depressed. A recent book of my own on a similar subject had not been nearly as successful, so watching the other author's celebrity was a bit like a root canal for my ego. My relative lack of success was in no way caused by the other author, and his success took nothing away from me, but I was nevertheless in a deep funk.

I also had a decision to make. As it turned out, he was having a book-signing party at a local Washington bookstore that evening. Should I go? The question made as much sense as: how would I like a hot, sharp stick poked in my eye?

But I thought about it.

Youth has its passion, but age has its bitterness, and, frankly, I didn't like the way it felt. First of all, it was pointless. What good did it do me to be depressed about someone else's success? It is one thing to be down about your own failure (although you shouldn't dwell on it), but what possible reason would you have to wallow in self-pity over someone else's good fortune? Wallowing didn't inspire me, it didn't change the sales figures for his book or mine; it did nothing but ruin my day and make me bitter, and bitterness has the double disadvantage of being both ugly and self-defeating. Did I really want to be that kind of a person? Worse yet, this could easily become a habit, because almost no one goes through life without having to deal with people who are more successful.

Sooner or later, you will have to deal with a sibling, a friend, or an acquaintance who makes the team when you don't, is named valedictorian, wins a tournament, gets a higher SAT score, dates a hotter girl or boy, gets into a better college, gets a better job, or buys a more expensive car or a better house, than you. Your reaction to all of this good fortune won't have the slightest effect on her or his success, but it will have a great deal to do with what a kind of a person you will become.

As I sat in the hotel room, I realized that I had a decision to make right there, and not just about whether I would go to the book signing. I had to decide whether I was going to be the sort of permanently small person who resents the successes of others. I could not control either this other author's sales or my own, but I could control how I reacted. I chose to get over it.

That night, I went to the signing, congratulated the author, shook his hand, and felt great about it. Life being what it is, there have been times when I've been tempted to be annoyed about someone else's good news, but I've frequently thought back on that afternoon.

Deciding not to let the successes of others bother you will mean you'll have one less annoyance to carry around; and like the decision not to join the ranks of the easily offended, it's actually quite liberating. The people with tight little bitter smiles and roiling intestines make up a club that you don't want to join.

This is also important in selecting friends. If you have any friends who resent your successes, you should recognize this obvious fact: they aren't really your friends in any sense of the word. (See the next rule.)

RULE 44

Your colleagues are not necessarily your friends, and your friends aren't your family.

Since you can't choose your family, choose your friends carefully. No matter how annoying they might seem to you these days, nothing replaces your family, because the most influential, most important people in your lives are your parents—not your friends, your teachers, or your coworkers. They will also be there when you need them, which isn't necessarily true of either friends or colleagues.

Because you spend so much time with them, the people who go to school or work with you can easily seem like friends or even members of an extended family. But relationships based on instant-messaging one another things like "wut up" and "CUL8R" ("see you later") or "DYJHIWSH" ("Don't You Just Hate It When S★ Happens?") are not necessarily profound or especially long-lasting. Most professional correspondence isn't much better, so it's a good idea not to mistake the relationship for something it is not.

Here's a nasty lesson in human nature: most people are governed by self-interest, so when the chips are down, people you imagine are your friends may let you down, if they aren't the ones planting the sharpened kitchen implements in your back.

Another (less cynical, perhaps) way of putting this is that your true friends will stand by you when you most need them, but the reality is that genuine courage and sacrifice are quite rare. Unless you recognize this, you could be in for a big shock.

This is one of the reasons to choose your friends as carefully as you choose a college; in some cases, that choice may be the same thing. In the eighteenth century Lord Chesterfield advised his son, "For it is a true saying *tell me who you live with and I will tell you who you are;* and it is equally true, that when a man of sense makes a friend of a knave or a fool he must have something bad to do, or to conceal."[168]

Your peer group has a chance to shape not just your character, but also your ambitions. Hang out with losers, and your chance of being a loser is enhanced; hang with skanks, and your skank quotient goes up; spend time with kids who take their futures seriously, and you are likely to do so as well. As a teaching institution, Harvard is actually not all it's cracked up to be: sometimes the classes are huge and the professors unavailable to undergraduates. But the real advantage and the great attraction of all of the top schools are the other students, the nation's most elite peer groups.

Seek out your own elite group.

RULE 45

Grown-ups forget how scary it is to be your age. Just re-member: this too will pass.

Unless you are a total screwup, your parents know that you will graduate, get a job, and be more or less OK. But you know there are losers who live in trailer parks or with their moms and work in dead-end jobs if they aren't junkies or unemployed. And you worry that you could end up being one of them. Whether or not you will depends on you.

You are about to undergo a series of transitions that might look familiar to your parents, but that look a lot sketchier to you: from high school to college; from college to grad school or a job—probably multiple jobs, possibly multiple careers; several changes of residence; relationships that may include marriage and the birth of children; the entire world of global competition, income, expenses, taxes, savings, and debt. The uncertainty and the explosion of choices, along with the shifting nature of the rules of life, make all of this especially intimidating. Not only is the future less predictable and the jobs and relationships less stable than in the past, you have also been given remarkably little in the way of a road map. Grown-ups in your life may have thought they were doing you a favor by not setting limits or answering you with harsh language like "no," but all of that simply makes life all the scarier. Somewhere at the back of your mind, you have probably realized that your expectations might exceed reality, and you are looking disillusionment in the face.

But the good news is that you can always turn it around. Life is full of successful former burnouts. Getting older, of course, does not necessarily mean becoming more mature, but it does provide a better sense of perspective—you'll learn that the bad stuff doesn't usually last. High school only lasts four years; your skin will clear up. No matter how bad your golf game was today, there's always tomorrow.

This works the other way around too: until you get older, you probably won't recognize your most valuable experiences. It could be the tough teacher you don't much like now, but who won't give up on you; the school that you can't wait to leave but that changes your life. Or the wrong choice that helps clarify the kind of person you don't want to be.

RULE 46

Check on the guinea pig in the basement.

This is another way of saying you should pay attention to the people and things around you. And this one is kind of personal. When I was younger, I had a guinea pig named Chester Pygge. I really wanted a dog, but I lived in a duplex that didn't allow them, and besides we didn't have the room. (I now have a house and two dogs.) In my search for a dog-substitute, I tried large turtles (they died), a parrot (who defecated all over the walls), and Chester.

I bought Chester a cage, filled it with nice-smelling wood chips, and even cut up a small cardboard box to serve as his pig house. He liked to sleep in the box, and I cut a door so that he could look out, which he seemed to like to do when he wasn't chewing the cardboard to pieces. (The chewing caused the house to fall down on him about every three or four days.) I regularly fed him his diet of pig pellets, which seemed bland, but which apparently went well with cardboard, and I made sure he had more-or-less-fresh water. Cleaning out the cage was another matter, and here we get to the part of the story I'm not really proud of.

After a few days, the wood shavings in Chester's cage would get extremely nasty, and I really hated having to clean them out. What made it worse was that I discovered that I was allergic to guinea pigs, so even a few minutes in the same room would bring on a sneezing jag and burning eyes. So I visited Chester less and less, and only when I had to, which was usually to feed him and give him a new box house. At that point in my life, I hadn't gotten used to changing diapers and barely cleaned up my own room, so cleaning Chester's cage was an ordeal I avoided as long as I could, even though I knew that it was my responsibility and that he was counting on me. As bad as the mess was for me, Chester actually had to live in it. Given their usual jobs, guinea pigs are used to putting up with a lot, especially from scientists and medical researchers. But even so, there are limits for even the most tolerant pig.

Chester lived to what I suppose was a ripe old age for pigs, but for years I had the same dream: I would suddenly realize that I had forgotten that I had a guinea pig in the basement. I had been going on with my life—going to work, watching television, going to ballgames—and had forgotten to go down to the basement for weeks. All that time, he was sitting there, without food, without water, in increasingly squalid conditions. And I had simply forgotten that he was down there all that time, day after day, week after week. In the dream, I was horrified and would rush down, but it was usually too late.

Of course, it was a guilt dream, and I had it coming.

But I think that dream—and it lasted for years—had a larger message. It wasn't just the guinea pig in the basement I had forgotten about. In my absorption in my career, my life, there were a lot of things I was forgetting and neglecting: parents, friends, children—all of the people who love you, rely on you, count on you, even when you are otherwise occupied.

Time passes quickly. You may not think about it now, but time is also passing for others in your life. For your grandmother, alone in a nursing home, who waits for a phone call or a visit; for a friend who may be alone in the hospital; or for a brother or sister just down the hall, lying awake in bed wrestling with a personal problem. Or maybe it's a parent who is going through a difficult period, losing a job, or being sick, while you hang out at the mall with your friends. They are all growing older, time is passing, even if you have forgotten all about them. You may not realize it yet, but even the smallest gesture will be appreciated, because you matter to other people far more than you really understand right now. You are not the only person who is lonely.

Look around. Whom have you forgotten?

Even if it cuts into your social life, even if it's inconvenient or hard, check on the guinea pig in the basement.

RULE 47

You are not perfect, and you don't have to be.

You might be tempted to look at the images of impossibly thin models, or celebrities with (apparently) perfect skin and six-pack abs, who hop on a Gulfstream jet to go shopping, and decide that your own body and maybe your whole life sucks.

But Celebrity World is a cartoonish fantasy: you inhabit the real world, where people occasionally have bad skin or a few extra pounds and have to drive their mom's Saturn to Wal-Mart. And that's OK, because it's reality and (almost) everybody else lives there too. Deal with it.

Apparently, though, a lot of young people are having a hard time with that. *Your Prom* magazine, for example, estimates that the average teenager now spends more than six hundred dollars on the prom. Searching for an explanation for the increasingly lavish price tag, the *Chicago Sun-Times* noted: "Today's teens are the first generation to grow up in perfection immersion: extreme makeovers, designer labels, unprecedented societal preoccupation with celebrity. Their expectations for prom are wildly inflated compared to those of their parents, who graduated in an era when limousines were for weddings, funerals and rich folks."[169]

But chasing perfection usually ends up in frustration, because somebody will always be doing more. Even in our zero-tolerance time, this applies to other areas of life as well, because sooner or later everybody screws up. Heroes stumble, champions have bad days, and even saints can get it wrong. But don't make the mistake of defining people solely by their flaws.

An Episcopal priest named John Hughes tells a story about his brief encounter with Mother Teresa in the mid-1980s.[170] Mother Teresa was already world-famous for her work with the poor, perhaps second only to the pope in the world of religious celebrity. Hughes and his wife were visiting Calcutta and helping care for destitute men at a home called Prem Dan.

Hughes admits that he was a bit starstruck at the prospect of meeting the famous nun. But during their visit, they had only caught brief glimpses of her and had become reconciled to the probability that they would never actually meet the extraordinary woman who had moved the world with her pleas for charity.

One day, about two weeks before they were scheduled to leave Calcutta, John was sitting in Prem Dan, changing the bandages on the men there. The process involved cutting off the old bandage, cleaning the wounds, applying Neosporin, and then reapplying the bandage.

While he was working, a nun sat down next to him, fingering her prayer beads. At first, Hughes thought it was his friend, a Sister Cyriac, and kept working. When he finally did look over, he found he was sitting only a few feet from Mother Teresa, who sat quietly, looking him directly in the eye.

Dumbstruck—he says that he "sort of blacked out momentarily"—Hughes recovered himself and then asked the most famous woman in the world if she'd like to help him. She would. Hughes cut off the dirty bandages, cleaned the sores, and applied the Neosporin, and Mother Teresa replaced the bandages and fastened each with a butterfly clip.

And here's where the story gets interesting.

Hughes noticed that Mother Teresa had done it wrong. She had put the butterfly clasp upside down on the bandage. "The elderly gent we were serving walked a short distance away as my realization sunk in. *I had just seen Mother Teresa make a mistake.*"

Hughes had to make a quick and extremely awkward decision. "Do you tell Martin Luther King, Jr., that he's made a grammatical mistake in the pulpit? Do you call Michael Jordan's attention to this traveling violation on his way to a thunderous dunk? Should I tell Mother Teresa, Nobel laureate, destined for sainthood, that she made a mistake in helping the poor?"

Hughes brought the man back and, pointing at the faulty clasp, told the saint that unless it was fixed, it would fall off. He told her she had put it on wrong.

"That world famous face—Mother Teresa's face—looked at what I was pointing to, listened to what I said, paused for several pregnant moments, and considered. My mind raced, telling me I must be wrong. She said, quietly, one word: 'Shoot.' Then she fixed the problem with the clasp."

Nothing about that story in any way diminishes the greatness of Mother Teresa; in fact, the story does rather the opposite. Hughes later wrote that the "images of the super-duper spirituality star were things in my mind, nothing more. The humble, human reality of who she was was greater than the media image, greater than the projections of the imagination."

The lesson here: even the most famous, most admired people in the world are, ultimately, human and fallible. George Washington lost battles; Abe Lincoln committed a series of political blunders; Brett Favre threw a lot of interceptions. The nitpickers of life will seize on the negative, maybe because it makes them more comfortable with their own mediocrity, but they get it backwards. The failings of the heroes are not grounds for cynicism; they remind us how extraordinary it is that ordinary people— parents, teachers, role models—do such extraordinary things.

RULE 48

Tell yourself the story of your life. Have a point.

Start by telling it up until now. What have you done so far?
Now go back and add in the bad stuff you left out—the rudeness, the lying, the petty betrayals, the bitchiness and thought-
lessness, all the stuff that, balanced with your good traits, tells
you how you are really coming along.

And now, imagine you are on your deathbed at a ripe old age
(and, yes, the odds are that you will actually be over forty someday). Look back on your life: What did you do? What will you
leave behind? What kind of a person were you? Do you want to
be remembered as a person of character and honesty? Of com-
passion and trustworthiness? Do you want your life to have made
a difference in the lives of others? And how are the decisions you
are making now contributing to or undermining those goals?

The important thing here is to see your life as a narrative,
a story that has a point to it, rather than a series of random,
pointless incidents. The decisions you make now won't just affect what happens next week, but may shape the rest of your
life. What feels good this Friday night might wreck your plans
for the next two decades.

Ask yourself: what do you want to be the meaning of your
life?

"Ultimately," wrote concentration camp survivor and psychia-
trist Viktor Frankl, "man should not ask what the meaning of

his life is, but rather must recognize that it is *he* who is asked. In a word, each man is questioned by life; and he can only answer to life by *answering for* his own life; to life he can only respond by being responsible."[171]

Steve Jobs, the CEO and cofounder of Apple and the Pixar animation studios, puts it somewhat differently: "Remembering that I'll be dead soon is the most important tool I've ever encountered to help me make the big choices in life."[172]

Speaking at Stanford University's 2005 commencement, the high-tech guru told the graduates that a year earlier he had been diagnosed with a potentially fatal cancer.

"I had a scan at 7:30 in the morning," he recalled, "and it clearly showed a tumor on my pancreas. I didn't even know what a pancreas was. The doctors told me this was almost certainly a type of cancer that is incurable, and that I should expect to live no longer than three to six months."

News like this tends to focus the mind wondrously, and Jobs was no exception, faced with the prospect that he would be dead within months.

Later that day, doctors performed a biopsy "where they stuck an endoscope down my throat, through my stomach and into my intestines, put a needle into my pancreas and got a few cells from the tumor." The news was good: Jobs would not die of an incurable disease; it turned out that he had a very rare form of the disease that was curable by surgery. "I had the surgery and I'm fine now," Jobs said. "This was the closest I've been to facing death, and I hope it's the closest I get for a few more decades."

But having lived through the prospect of dying, Jobs told the Stanford grads:

> *I can now say this to you with a bit more certainty than when death was a useful but purely intellectual concept: No one wants to die. Even people who want to go to heaven don't want to die to get there. And yet death is the destination we all share. No one has ever escaped it. And that is as it should be, because Death is very likely the single best invention of Life. It*

is Life's change agent. It clears out the old to make way for the new. Right now the new is you, but someday not too long from now, you will gradually become the old and be cleared away. Sorry to be so dramatic, but it is quite true.

His message: "Your time is limited, so don't waste it living someone else's life. . . ."

Unfortunately, he followed that up with a series of New Age clichés, but the point was important anyway: you need to think about your life, because it is up to you what it will be about.

Having survived the Nazi death camps, Frankl concluded that "it did not really matter what we expected from life, but rather what life expected from us."

"Our answer," he wrote, "must consist, not in talk and meditation, but in right action and in right conduct. Life ultimately means taking the responsibility to find the right answer to its problems and to fulfill the tasks which it constantly sets for each individual."[173]

What does life expect of you?

RULE 49

Don't forget to say thank you.

As often as you say, "It's my life," the fact is that it's not, at least not yet and not exclusively. You hold the lives of others in your own as well. Remember that you matter to others because what you do affects them more deeply than you probably can guess right now.

You cannot begin to imagine how much time, effort, and love have gone into raising you since the miraculous moment of your birth: changing your diapers; feeding you baby food that you spit all over your bib; reading you to sleep; watching your first step; taking you to the bus for the first day of school; making you dinner; buying you clothes; dressing you; cleaning up after you; shopping for your Christmas presents; helping you with homework; bandaging the cuts; building those silly dioramas the night before they are due; signing you up for swimming lessons; taking you to the doctor for your ear infection; the family road trips where you asked, "Are we there yet?" fifty thousand times; driving you to lessons and games in the minivan; attending your soccer games, concerts, band performances, and parent-teacher conferences; paying for your braces; hearing you say you hate them; helping you with your first date; lying awake at night worrying; graduations; saving for your college tuition; the anxieties, fears, and moments of incredible satisfaction, surprise, hope, and pride.

It wouldn't hurt to show some gratitude.

Spoiled brats think they had all of this coming as a matter of right, so they miss the remarkable gift they have been given. It may not even occur to them to say thanks.

For those of you who have a better sense of what you owe, the problem is more difficult. Just how do you say thank you for a life and for a lifetime of gifts and service? How do you pay it back? Somehow, a Hallmark card just doesn't cut it.

My favorite story of gratitude is Anatole France's story of the juggler who wants more than anything to show his devotion and gratitude to Mary, the Mother of Jesus.[174]

The juggler was named Barnabas, and he lived in the days of King Louis and traveled from town to town entertaining crowds with his skill and showmanship. Eventually, he joined a monastery and became a monk, hoping to be of service to the Virgin.

He grew despondent, however, when he saw how little he had to offer compared to the other monks. Everyone else had a special talent or skill that he devoted to praising Mary. The prior, for example, wrote learned books; Brother Maurice copied his treatises onto parchment with a beautiful hand; Brother Alesandre illuminated the manuscripts with delicate miniatures representing the Blessed Virgin; Brother Marbode was a skilled sculptor, while others among the monks composed beautiful poetry and hymns to honor the Mother of God.

Seeing all of this, Barnabas felt his inadequacy. In contrast to the learned, talented monks around him, he was an ignorant and simple man who could not even hope to make the sort of beautiful gifts that his fellow monks offered. He couldn't deliver a sermon, or write a learned treatise on theology, or carve a statue. "Alas," he said, "I have nothing."

"Thus," wrote Anatole France, "did he lament and abandon himself to his misery."

Until one morning when he had an idea. He got up from his cot and ran to the chapel and remained there alone for an hour.

The next day he was back in the chapel, and, in fact, he began disappearing into it frequently, going there whenever he was free and the chapel was empty. This naturally aroused the curiosity of his fellow monks, who wondered what he was doing in the chapel by himself.

Since it was his job to check into such things, the prior decided to follow Barnabas, and one night went to the chapel accompanied by two other monks. They looked through the bars to see what Barnabas was doing.

And there was Barnabas before the image of the Virgin, "his head on the floor and his feet in the air, juggling with six copper balls and twelve knives."

Barnabas had realized that, after all, he did have a gift for Mary; he showed his gratitude by giving her the very best that he had. He was not a poet, or a sculptor, or an artist. He was a juggler, so he juggled.

You may not grow up to be a CEO, or a brain surgeon, or an opera singer. But whatever work you undertake, do it well, with skill and pride.

That's how you pay it back.

RULE 50

Enjoy this while you can.

Sure parents are a pain, school's a bother, and life is depressing. Someday you'll realize how wonderful it was to be a kid.

It's over too soon—summer, high school, life. Blink and it will be gone. Savor it.

Maybe you should start now.

appendix I

FOURTEEN RULES KIDS
WON'T LEARN IN SCHOOL

By Charles J. Sykes

1. Life is not fair. Get used to it.

The average teenager uses the phrase "It's not fair" 8.6 times a day. The kids got it from their parents, who said it so often they decided they must be the most idealistic generation ever. When the parents started hearing it from their own kids, they realized Rule 1.

2. The real world won't care as much as your school does about your self-esteem.

It'll expect you to accomplish something before you feel good about yourself. This may come as a shock. When inflated self-esteem meets reality, most kids complain that it's not fair. (See Rule 1.)

3. Sorry, you won't make forty thousand dollars a year right out of high school.

And you won't be a vice president or have a car phone either. You may even have to wear a uniform that doesn't have a Gap label.

4. If you think your teacher is tough, wait until you get a boss.

He doesn't have tenure, so he tends to be a bit edgier. When you screw up, he's not going to ask you how you FEEL about it.

5. Your school may have done away with winners and losers. Life hasn't.

In some schools, they'll give you as many times as you want to get the right answer. Failing grades have been abolished and class valedictorians scrapped, lest anyone's feelings be hurt. Effort is as important as results. This, of course, bears not the slightest resemblance to anything in real life. (See Rules 1, 2, and 4.)

6. Flipping burgers is not beneath your dignity.

Your grandparents had a different word for burger flipping. They called it opportunity. They weren't embarrassed making minimum wage either. They would have been embarrassed to sit around talking about Kurt Cobain all weekend.

7. Television is not real life.

Your life is not a sitcom. Your problems will not all be solved in thirty minutes, minus time for commercials. In real life people actually have to leave the coffee shop to go to jobs.

8. Before you were born, your parents weren't as boring as they are now.

They got that way paying your bills, cleaning up your room, and listening to you tell them how idealistic you are. And by the way, before you save the rain forest from the blood-sucking parasites of your parents' generation, try delousing the closet in your bedroom.

9. Life is not divided into semesters. And you don't get summers off.

Not even Easter break. They expect you to show up every day. For eight hours. And you don't get a new life every ten weeks. It just goes on and on. While we're at it, few jobs are interested in fostering your self-expression or helping you find yourself. Fewer still lead to self-realization. (See Rules 1 and 2.)

10. It's not your parents' fault. If you screw up, you are responsible.

This is the flip side of "It's my life," and "You're not the boss of me," and other eloquent proclamations of your generation. When you turn eighteen, it's on your dime. Don't whine about it, or you'll sound like a baby boomer.

11. Be nice to nerds.

You may end up working for them. We all could.

12. Smoking does not make you look cool. . . . It makes you look moronic.

13. You are not immortal.

(See Rule 9.) If you are under the impression that living fast, dying young, and leaving a beautiful corpse are romantic, you obviously haven't seen one of your peers at room temperature lately.

14. Enjoy this while you can.

Sure parents are a pain, school's a bother, and life is depressing. Someday you'll realize how wonderful it was to be a kid. Maybe you should start now.

endnotes

1. Christina Hoff Sommers and Sally Satel, *One Nation Under Therapy* (New York: St. Martin's Press, 2005).

2. Jean Twenge, *Generation Me* (New York: Free Press, 2006).

3. Michael Barone, *Hard America, Soft America* (New York: Crown Forum, 2004).

4. James Stenson, *Upbringing: A Discussion Handbook for Parents of Young Children* (Princeton, N.J.: 2004).

5. Jonathan Yardley, "Read No Evil: A Textbook Case of Censorship," *The Washington Post* (June 12, 2003).

6. Hara Estroff Marano, "A Nation of Wimps," *Psychology Today* (November/December 2004).

7. Michael Barone, op. cit., 13.

8. C. S. Lewis, *The Screwtape Letters* (New York: Bantam Books, 1982), 75.

9. Sam Dillon, "Literacy Falls for Graduates From College, Testing Finds," *The New York Times* (December 16, 2005).

10. "New Study of The Literacy of College Students Finds Some Are Graduating With Only Basic Skills," American Institutes for Research (January 2006); "Study: Most College Students Lack Skills," Associated Press (January 19, 2006).

11. "Parents, students, don't see a crisis over science and math," *USA Today* (February 14, 2006).

12. "Skills Gap Report—A Survey of the American Manufacturing Workforce," National Association of Manufacturers (December 19, 2005).

13. Ibid.

14. H. L. Mencken, *A Second Mencken Chrestomathy,* edited by Terry Teachout (New York: Alfred A. Knopf, 1995), 303.

15. Viktor E. Frankl, *Man's Search for Meaning* (New York: Washington Square Press, 1984), 86.

16. All quotes are from Hawking's personal Web site: http://www.hawking.org.uk/text/disable/disable.html.

17. Hara Estroff Marano, op. cit.

18. Charles Sykes, "The Rise of the Ninny State," *CNI Newspapers;* available at: http://www.620wtmj.com/_content/talk/charliesykes/index.asp?id=8&entry=4050.

19. Naomi Aoki, "Harshness of red marks has students seeing purple," *The Boston Globe* (August 23, 2004).

20. Charles Sykes, op. cit.

21. Farm school blog (August 15, 2005), http://farm schoolathome.blogspot.com/2005/08/swimming-lessons-and-rumplestiltskin.html.

22. Roy E. Baumeister, Jennifer D. Campbell, Joachim I. Krueger, and Kathleen D. Vohs, "Exploding the Self-Esteem Myth," *Scientific American* (December 20, 2004).

23. Sommers and Satel, op. cit., 31.

24. Baumeister, et. al., op. cit.

25. Baumeister, et. al., op. cit.

26. Martha Irvine, "Young workers want it all, now: Oh, and they'll need to take next Friday off, too," Associated Press (June 27, 2005).

27. Patrik Jonsson, "Haven't scored the good life yet? Hire a coach!" *The Christian Science Monitor* (June 5, 2006).

28. Ibid.

29. "Professors of Education: It's How You Learn, Not What You Learn, That's Most Important" Public Agenda (October 22, 1997).

30. Stephanie Armour, "Generation Y: They've arrived at work with a new attitude," *USA Today* (November 7, 2005).

31. James Stenson, op. cit., 106–7.

32. Michelle Moran, "Grading the Generation Curve," *The Gourmet Retailer* (February 1, 2005).

33. "Targeting Teens," Business Analysis and Research Department, Newspaper Association of America (October 2005).

34. "Thirty & Broke" *Business Week* (November 4, 2005).

35. Ibid.

36. "Teens come up short on financial literacy," Associated Press (April 6, 2006); see also: Tom O'Neill, "Teens flunk personal finance quiz," *The Cincinnati Post* (April 6, 2006); and "Financial Literacy Shows Slight Improvement Among Nation's High School Students," at www.jumpstart.org.

37. Olivia Barker, "Coming-of-age grows lavish," *USA Today* (April 19, 2006).

38. "Hyatt Resorts Launches 'HyaTTeen Suite 16' Luxury Slumber Party—from Limo Rides to Lounging Pool-Side, Teens Celebrate In Style," Hospitality Net (May 2, 2006).

39. Jaimee Rose, "Welcome to Marissa's World," *The Arizona Republic* (April 26, 2006).

40. Ibid.

41. "An Assessment of Survey Data on Attitudes About Teaching, "Public Agenda (August 25, 2003).

42. "Do Students Have Too Much Homework?", A Report by The Brown Center on Education (October 2003).

43. "Getting By: What American Teenagers Really Think About Their Schools," Public Agenda (February 11, 1997).

44. Michael Crowley, "That's Outrageous! Expel These Teachers," *Readers' Digest* (September 2005).

45. Sol Stern, "Dance of the Lemons," *The City Journal* (autumn 1998).

46. John Stossel, "Stupid in America: Why your kids are probably dumber than Belgians," *Reason* (January 13, 2006).

47. Ibid.

48. Sommers and Satel, op. cit., 5.

49. Nicole C. Wong, "New Relaxation badge is a hit with preteen scouts," *Knight-Ridder Newspapers* (April 23, 2002).

50. Ibid.

51. Families and Work Institute, "What's Special About Me?", http://www.familiesandwork.org/911ah/lp_prek-2_mu.html.

52. "Guidelines for Addressing the Needs of Students in the Aftermath of Trauma," United Federation of Teachers and NYC Board of Education (2001), http://www.uft.org/member/workplace/school/guidelines_for_/index.html.

53. Sommers and Satel, op. cit., 216.

54. Glynn Custred, "Onward to Adequacy," *Academic Questions* (summer 1990).

55. "Different Drummers: How Teachers of Teachers View Public Education," Public Agenda (1997).

56. Mark Mlawer, "My Kid Beat Up Your Honor Student," *Education Week* (July 13, 1994).

57. Mike Weiss, "What happens when everyone's a winner," *The Boston Globe* (February 23, 2006).

58. Melinda Henneberger, "New Gym Class: No More Choosing Up Sides," *The New York Times* (May 16, 1993).

59. "Dodgeball: Whip It Good: The growing debate over 'murderball,'" http://www.brainevent.com/be/TheNews/head_to_head/20010604.

60. Neil Seeman, "Dodge This: Banning dodgeball is like banning childhood," National Review Online (May 4, 2001).

61. Ibid.

62. Neil F. Williams, "The Physical Education Hall of Shame," *The Journal of Physical Education, Recreation & Dance* 63, no. 6 (1992).

63. Rick Reilly, "The Weak Shall Inherit the Gym," *Sports Illustrated* (May 8, 2001).

64. Chris Kahn, "In the pursuit of safety, teeter-totters and swings are disappearing from playgrounds," Orlando *Sun-Sentinel* (July 18, 2005).

65. Sandy Louey, "Recess Gets Regulated," *Sacramento Bee* (August 22, 2004).

66. Martin Miller, "At This School, 'It' Is a Touchy Subject," *Los Angeles Times* (June 12, 2002).

67. Dan Uhlinger, "Towns' Worst Fears Realized: Suits Follow Playground Mishaps," *Hartford Courant* (September 24, 1999).

68. Greg Toppo, "The great American swing set is teetering," *USA Today* (March 20, 2006).

69. Chris Kahn, op. cit.

70. Patricia Biederman, "Tossing Self-Esteem into the Mix," *Los Angeles Times* (May 9, 2001).

71. Sean Murphy, "Mom makes teen stand on street with sign," Associated Press (November 16, 2005).

72. "Estimated Probability of Competing in Athletics Beyond the High School Interscholastic Level," National College Athletic Association (2005).

73. Gary Emerling, "Virginia schools ban game shake to curb fighting," *The Washington Times* (November 11, 2005).

74. Patricia Dalton, "What's Wrong With This Outfit, Mom?" *The Washington Post* (November 20, 2005).

75. Blog entry in "Sex and the Mil-town" (March 25, 2006), http://satcmke.blogspot.com/2006/04/fashion-faux-pas.html.

76. Patricia Dalton, op. cit.

77. Ibid.

78. See S. Mark Wilson, "Income Mobility and the Fallacy of Class-Warfare Arguments Against Tax Relief," The Heritage Foundation (March 8, 2001).

79. Ben Wildavsky, "McJobs: Inside America's Largest Youth Training Program," *Policy Review* (summer 1989).

80. Ibid.

81. Katherine S. Newman, *No Shame in My Game* (New York: First Vintage Books/Russell Sage Foundation, 2000).

82. Ben Wildavsky, op. cit.

83. P. J. O'Rourke, *All the Trouble in the World: The Lighter Side of Overpopulation, Famine, Ecological Disaster, Ethnic Hatred, Plague, and Poverty* (New York: Atlantic Monthly Press, 1994), 9.

84. P. J. O'Rourke, *Peace Kills* (New York: Atlantic Monthly Press, 2004), 130–31.

85. Ibid., 136.

86. Rob Walker, "Notes from the Brand Underground," *The New York Times Magazine* (July 30, 2006).

87. See Justin Pope, "Colleges try to deal with hovering parents," Associated Press (August 28, 2005); and Samuel G. Freedman, "Weaning Parents From Children As They Head Off to College," *The New York Times* (September 15, 2004).

88. Hara Estroff Marano, "A Nation of Wimps," op. cit.

89. Ibid.

90. Ibid.

91. Ibid.

92. Sue Shellenbarger, "Helicopter Parents Go to Work: Moms And Dads Are Now Hovering at the Office," *The Wall Street Journal* (March 16, 2006).

93. "Nose piercing means trouble for Wisconsin eighth-grader," Associated Press (March 22, 2006).

94. "Woods apologizes for 'spaz' comment," Reuters (April 13, 2006).

95. Rick Esenberg, blog entry, "Tiger Woods had less than optimal muscle control," http://sharkandshepherd.blogspot.com/2006/O4/tiger-woods-had-less-than-optimal_13.html.

96. Damon Rose, "The S-word," BBC News (April 12, 2006).

97. Edward Abbey, *The Fool's Progress* (New York: Avon Books, 1988), 39.

98. Nisha Ramachandran, "The parent trap: boomerang kids," *U.S. News and World Report* (December 12, 2005).

99. Anna Bahney, "The Bank of Mom and Dad," *The New York Times* (April 20, 2006).

100. Frank F. Furstenberg, Sheela Kennedy, Vonnie C. McLoyd, Ruben G. Rumbaut, and Richard A. Setterstein, Jr., "Growing up is harder to do," *Contexts,* American Sociological Association, vol. 3, no. 3 (summer 2004).

101. Ibid.

102. Megan Twohey, "The coming-back kid," *Milwaukee Journal Sentinel* (May 10, 2006).

103. "Johnny Lechner, Professional Student—Afflicted with On-Set Career Crisis, Says Gen Y Career Coach," PRWEB (May 5, 2006).

104. Theodore Dalrymple, *Life at the Bottom: The Worldview That Makes the Underclass* (Chicago: Ivan R. Dee, 2001), 10.

105. Tom McMahon, blog entry, "Love Acts the Part," at http://www.tommcmahon.net/2005/06/love_acts_the_p.html.

106. Philip K. Dick, from http://www.quotationsbook .com/quotes/33542/view.

107. Michael Barone, op. cit.

108. H. L. Mencken, *A Mencken Chrestomathy* (New York: Knopf, 1949), 626.

109. "The Ethics of American Youth," The Josephson Institute of Ethics (2004).

110. Rebecca Hagelin, "Taking Back Our Homes," *Imprimis* (April 2006).

111. "UK Children Go Online: Final Report," London School of Economics (April 2005).

112. Robert E. Rector, Kirk A. Johnson, Lauren R. Noyes, and Martin Shannan, "The Harmful Effects of Early Sexual Activity and Multiple Sexual Partners Among Women," The Heritage Foundation (June 2003); see also: "Sexually Active Teenagers Are More Likely to Be Depressed and Commit Suicide," The Heritage Foundation (June 2003).

113. François, Duc de La Rochefoucauld, *Maxims,* (London: Penguin, 1959), 65.

114. Judith Martin, from http://www.brainyquote.com/ quotes/quotes/j/judithmart161215.html.

115. Linda Clawson, "Schools to change policy," *Milwaukee Journal Sentinel* (June 27, 1996).

116. "N.J. kindergartners suspended for threats during playground 'cops and robbers,'" AP/Court TV (April 6, 2000).

117. "Girl doodles her way into 3-day suspension," Associated Press (May 5, 2002).

118. See Zero Intelligence Net (October 17, 2004), http://www.zerointelligence.net/archives/000442.php.

119. For a comprehensive look at zero-tolerance policies, see www.overlawyered.com; see also: Neal Boortz, "Zero-tolerance—zero thought," Townhall.com (June 4, 2004).

120. H. L. Mencken, *A Mencken Chrestomathy* (New York: Knopf, 1949), 616.

121. William J. Booher, "Boy turns in knife but may still be expelled," *The Indianapolis Star* (April 3, 2006).

122. "Georgia girl's Tweety Bird chain runs afoul of weapons policy," CNN.com (September 28, 2000).

123. Ibid.

124. "School board votes to expel student for possessing Advil on campus," National School Boards Association Web site, Legal Clips (December 2003).

125. "Asthma heroine branded 'drug dealer,'" BBC News (May 5, 1998).

126. "CBS alters Couric photo to slim her down," Associated Press (August 30, 2006).

127. Kate Jackson, "0 is the new 8: As waistlines grow, women's clothing sizes shrink incredibly," *The Boston Globe,* (May 5, 2006).

128. Lance Burri, blog entry, "The Thanksgiving Column" (November 26, 2004), at http://lanceburri.blogspot.com/2004/11/thanksgiving-day-column.html.

129. Paul Graham, "Why Nerds Are Unpopular" (February 2003), at http://www.paulgraham.com/nerds.html.

130. Ibid.

131. Del Jones, "CEOs say how you treat a waiter can predict a lot about character," *USA Today* (April 17, 2006).

132. Denis Waitley, from http://www.brainyquote.com/quotes/quotes/d/deniswaitl130424.html.

133. Vince Lombardi, from http://www.brainyquote.com/quotes/quotes/v/vincelomba130581.html.

134. Alfie Kohn, "The Case Against Competition," *Working Mother* (September 1987).

135. Vince Lombardi, from http://www.brainyquote .com/quotes/quotes/v/vincelomba151250.html.

136. Quoted by Greg Moran, "The Circle Game" (January 1999), at http://www.tennisserver.com/circlegame/circlegame_ 99_01.html; Kohn frequently writes and speaks about the evils of musical chairs; see, for example: "No Contest," *New Age Journal* (September/October 1986).

137. Jim Litke, "Bode Miller on 0 for 5 Olympic Bust: Man, I Rocked Here. . . ." Associated Press (February 25, 2006).

138. Bill Saporito, "How Bode Got Booted," *Time* (February 14, 2006).

139. Theodore Roosevelt, "The Man in the Arena," speech at the Sorbonne, Paris, France, (April 23, 1910).

140. Mike Royko, "A Discrimination Charge Hits Bottom," *Chicago Tribune* (May 22, 1991).

141. Michael Y. Park, "Ailing Man Sues Fast-Food Firms," Fox News (July 24, 2002), http://www.foxnews.com/story/ 0,2933,58652,00.html; see also: "Fast Food: Give Me My Million," at http://www.overlawyered.com/archives/000029.html, and http://www.foxnews.com/story/0,2933,58652,00.html.

142. James K. Glassman, "From Parody to Reality," Tech Central Station (May 21, 2003).

143. Michael Krauss, "Today's Tort Suits Are Stranger Than Fiction," Virginia Viewpoint (May 2003), http://www .virginiainstitute.org/viewpoint/2003_05.html.

144. Ibid.

145. Guy Barnett, "Time for a Fat Fight," *The Herald Sun* (July 17, 2002) (quoting Ralph Nader).

146. "CSPI And Brownell: Two Twinkies In One Package," The Center for Consumer Freedom (June 4, 2002), http:// www.consumerfreedom.com/news_detail.cfm/headline/1441; see also: biography of Bronwell at http://www.activistcash .com/biography.cfm/bid/1289.

147. "Trial Lawyers Still Looking for a Drive-Thru Payday," The Center for Consumer Freedom (May 12, 2003), at http:// www.consumerfreedom.com/news_detail.cfm/headline/1915.

148. "Public Health Activists vs. Consumer Freedom: Video Highlights," The Center for Consumer Freedom (December 4, 2003), at http://www.consumerfreedom.com/news_detail.cfm/headline/2248.

149. "Thompson's take on fat," *Milwaukee Journal Sentinel* (July 9, 2003); see also: Charles Sykes, "Tommy, may I? Or How Tommy Became Nanny-in-Chief," *Isthmus* (July 17, 2003), available at http://www.620wtmj.com/_content/talk/charliesykes/index.asp?id=8&entry=1795.

150. Don Behm and Lawrence Sussman, "Beer was the fuel in crash that killed 5," *Milwaukee Journal Sentinel* (August 29, 2005).

151. Mike Nichols, "Beer-can memorial a slap in the face," *Milwaukee Journal Sentinel* (August 29, 2005).

152. "Generation M: Media in the Lives of 8–18 Year-olds," The Kaiser Family Foundation (March 2005).

153. Ibid.

154. See Claudia Wallis, "The Multitasking Generation," *Time* (March 27, 2006).

155. Ibid.

156. Hara Estroff Marano, "A Nation of Wimps," op. cit.

157. "Generation M: Media in the Lives of 8–18 Year-olds," op. cit.

158. Philip Dormer Stanhope, 4th earl of Chesterfield (1694–1773); *Lord Chesterfield's Letters,* letter, May 11, 1752, to his son, Philip Stanhope, 4th earl, Esq., 5th ed., vol. 3, (London, 1774), 304.

159. Sharon Jayson, "Tech creates a bubble for kids," *USA Today* (June 20, 2006).

160. Philip Dormer Stanhope, op. cit., letter (October 9, 1746).

161. Philip Dormer Stanhope, op. cit., letter, (September 5, 1748).

162. "Best of the Web," Opinion Journal (February 17, 2006), http://www.opinionjournal.com/best/?id=110007988.

163. National Assessment of Education Progress 200 History Report Card, http://nces.ed.gov/nationsreportcard/ushis-

tory/results/; see also: Diane Ravitch, "Statement on NAEP 2001 U.S. History Report Card (May 9, 2002), http://www.nagb.org/naep/history_ravitch.html.

164. Sam Dillon, "From Yale to Cosmetology School, Americans Brush Up on History and Government," *The New York Times* (September 16, 2005).

165. "Simpsons 'trump' First Amendment," BBC News (March 1, 2006).

166. Quoted in Jonathan Yardley, op. cit., from Diane Ravitch, *The Language Police: How Pressure Groups Restrict What Students Learn* (New York: Alfred A. Knopf, 2003).

167. Peter Kreeft, *A Refutation of Moral Relativism* (San Francisco: Ignatius Press, 1999), 85.

168. *Lord Chesterfield's Letters,* op. cit.

169. Leslie Baldacci, "Not just a 3-hour dance," *Chicago Sun-Times* (May 23, 2006).

170. John Hughes, "Mother," from *Broken-Winged Flights,* © John Hughes, 1998.

171. Viktor Frankl, *Man's Search for Meaning* (New York: Simon and Schuster, 1963), 172.

172. The full text of Jobs's speech can be found at http://news-service.stanford.edu/news/2005/june15/jobs-061505.html.

173. Viktor E. Frankl, op. cit., 98.

174. Anatole France, "Our Lady's Juggler," can be found at http://www.bibliomania.com/0/5/207/592/8151/1/frameset.html.